MANNERS MATTER

TRANSFORMING LIFE THROUGH ETIQUETTE.

KIRYOWA IDRISA

Made with ♥ on the Notion Press Platform
www.notionpress.com

I dedicate this book to ***YOU***.

To YOU the unsung heroes of everyday kindness;

To YOU (those) who choose respect over rudeness;

To YOU the gentle souls who weave harmony in our lives;

And to YOU (all) who believe in the transformative power of good manners and etiquette.

This book is for YOU.

May your light continue to shine bright and inspire others to follow the noble path of respect, understanding, and human decency.

Contents

Preface

In our daily lives, we often hear terms like code of conduct, procedure, manners, mores, rules, and many others that are used interchangeably to describe social, official, and professional behavior.

All these sets of norms, rules, codes, and manners are what distinguish us from animals in one way or another.

While not all manners, behaviors, or morals are universally acceptable, some are fundamental and cut across all societies and communities, regardless of country or race.

By definition, etiquette is the set of norms of personal behavior in polite society, functioning as an ethical code of the expected or accepted social behavior within a given society.

Manners Matter: *Transforming Life Through Etiquette* delves into the significant role that etiquette plays in the tapestry of human relationships. These principles act as the threads that weave interactions together, fostering respect, understanding, and harmony. This book emphasizes how cultivating good etiquette in various sectors of life—religion, personal growth, social interactions, professional success, and relationships—can lead to a more fulfilling and respectful existence.

As the author, I bring a unique perspective shaped by my diverse background in Food Technology, Health Sciences, and Biotechnology, and my extensive travels across the globe, including Egypt, Poland, Germany, USA, Russia, and India. My passion for sustainability and my role as a global member of the American Society for Microbiology have further enriched my understanding of the interconnectedness of our actions and the importance of ethical behavior.

Manners Matter serves as an essential guide to cultivating the principles of good manners and etiquette. It provides practical insights into how these principles can transform everyday interactions into meaningful and respectful experiences. The book highlights the profound impact that etiquette has on personal growth, social interactions, professional success, and relationships.

Through engaging anecdotes and practical tips, this book illustrates how mastering etiquette can transform one's life. You will discover practical ways to embody etiquette in various life sectors, ensuring that you not only improve your social skills but also make a positive impact on the world around you.

It is my hope that this book will inspire **YOU** to reflect on your behavior, embrace the principles of etiquette, and strive to cultivate respect, understanding, and harmony in all your interactions. Remember, the journey towards personal growth and ethical behavior is a continuous one, and by taking smaller steps consistently, we can achieve bigger dreams.

Let us embark on this journey together and transform our lives through the power of good manners and etiquette.

Thank you for embarking on this journey with us. Let the principles of etiquette guide you towards a more respectful, understanding, and harmonious life.

K. Idrisa (Author), Dynamic Writer | Public Speaker | Food Technologist | Sustainability Advocate.

ONE

ETIQUETTE.

The word ***etiquette*** *has often been used to refer to good behavior in any society; thus, it refers to* ***social*** *and* ***ethical*** *guidelines that control how a responsible individual must behave in a society or community. From allowing us "****Humans****" to interact with each other and society as respectful and polite individuals to understanding how nature and the ecosystem works. Etiquette is not just about* ***rules, norms, codes of conduct****, or* ***morals*** *we must follow but a way of showing respect, consideration, and appreciation for others and the ecosystem as well. From a seconf person's point of view, different etiquette has been induced, such as social etiquette, which tells an individual how to behave in society and amongst people of given genera;* ***corporate etiquette****, which is for professional and work and the individual is ordained to maintain the decorum of the organization or workforce they are in. Wedding,* *meeting, bathroom, telephone, eating, and business etiquette have also been coined in different communities to set a specific code for which people must interact.*

The ability of one to politely inform others about their being late for a given meeting as soon as possible is a form of professionalism; however, from an ethical point of view, it symbolizes respect. Respecting others regardless of their class, origin, or race is one of ***life's highest*** *forms of etiquette. People's space, beliefs, opinions, and time must always be respected for a better society. Being punctual is one way to respect people's time, and prior notice about being late, postponed events, or preponed events is also a good way to show respect to people's time regardless of their class or level in a given community setting or organization. Beliefs and opinions are often the causatives of misunderstandings and divisions amongst people in a given society.*

Thus, showing respect, positivity, and understanding towards one's beliefs and opinions is a high form of etiquette. Even though you disagree with someone, respecting their opinions and beliefs helps understand their perspective. Many people have been sieved by their table manners which literally portray one's degree of ethical behavior and morals.

Differences in cultures, religions, norms, and hierarchy occur as we move from one place to another, but table etiquettes are more similar among all. Talking with food in one's mouth is globally considered bad table etiquette; in some societies, washing dishes or cleaning the table after eating is considered moral, while in some societies, it is neutral. Gratitude and appreciation, as being polite and soft to others, are considered good codes of conduct globally. Saying "please" in any language and "thank you" are simple but effective ways to show appreciation to others. Sending thank you notes to people who have gifted anything in some societies is mandatory and considered gift etiquette, while in others, it's neutral.

Importance of Etiquettes and Mastering them in different aspects of life.

The principles and values that govern one's behavior and decision-making fall under five different types of ethical and moral classes or sections, i.e., ***religious, personal, social, professional, and relationship ethics****. These all have different importance in one's life, and they might be sequential or complex with each other. Religious etiquettes are profound and render a person's ability to make informed decisions with regard to their religion and beliefs. Any person's moral and spiritual life gives them a sense of belonging, direction, and purpose in life. Most world religions (monotheism or polytheism) have an ultimate belief in the supernatural being (s) who created them and laid down specific codes of practice and worship to follow, and deviance is considered a* ***sin****.*

While a few people who do not have such beliefs also have special beliefs which make them have compassion, humility, devotion, and portray forgiveness and empathy to others in a given community. These all bring about harmony and respect in a given community and society. Having a sense of purpose allows people to understand that nature and the ecosystem are bound together; thus, prayer and supplications help us to interconnect with all the beings in the universe and the greatest supernatural. Things such as ***honesty, integrity, responsibility, and empathy*** *fall in a broad group of etiquettes called,* ***Personal ethics****. This help defines and enlighten someone's character and personality with respect to the values and norms of a given society. It is important for one to have the highest and most exquisite personal ethics.*

*This is because, by the character definition and portrayal to the society, one can be seen as a threat or welcoming. Many people whose personal ethics are poor have been cast out of different societies, and some have been accused of crimes against humanity. Incidences of rape, murder, child abuse, torture, and many other inhuman activities have been implicated in the loss of personal ethics in society and the demise of religious ethics as well. Saings have it that, "****the only way to judge a man's character is by observing their personal etiquette; they tell a lot more about them than what they talk about themselves****". Socially, a person must abide by and portray certain behavior or morals in a given society they are confined to. Most social etiquettes are not inborn or assimilated by the environment, but rather the community and the environment nurture them as they grow up.*

Because of these differences in social ethics, people can be known to belong to certain groups or societies, such as Asians, Americans, Europeans, or even African societies. A quick example is a washroom and toilet morals; they differ from continent to continent where. Asians will always use water in the toilet, and others might prefer toilet paper, while a few might not use any. One cannot learn this social behavior without interaction and getting nurtured by the environment where the behavior is practiced and accepted. These ethics promote social cohesion and help us to build a just and equitable society. These normally include justice, respect for diversity, and environmental responsibility. Education, whether formal or informal, will always lead us to have a specific field of work or area of the profession we all fall in.

The etiquette governing professional growth and success is always important in one's line of work or duty. It aids in one maintaining a professional standard and promotes trust, respect, and integrity among colleagues and clients at work or business. Values such as confidentiality, objectivity, competence, and fairness are key in developing a well-diverse and robust professional, ethical code for anyone. Imagine having a coffee shop where workers come at any time they desire and in any attire they want. Sometimes, these workers might not come to work, making losses in your business, of which the owner or entrepreneur will have to suffer the consequences. Thus, if the coffee shop owner sets up specific standards regarding arrival time and procedure of absence, this can be reduced. The business can sustain itself further and keep serving the public.

*Relationships, surely a lot happens in relationships regardless of the type of relationship and how many people are participating in it. The term relationship covers a broad range of affairs from family, friends, lovers, and enemies as well. Having sound ethical principles for the different types of relationships, one is involved in is a great way to understand life and keep a smile on your face as well. Some relationships might be toxic, others calming, and others, such as family and children, are mandatory. Creating trust, honesty, good communication, and commitment in any particular relationship helps one to prioritize different things and quickly have the ability to make informed decisions in a relationship. People tend to ignore the effects of relationships in their course to success, but they often forget the third law of motion, "**For every action, there is an equal and opposite reaction**." Hence at some point in time, the effects of these relationships might uplift or hinder your way to success.*

TWO
RELIGION

Religion and, in most cases, beliefs walk-in handy. Most people have these two ingrained in their identity, and they help shape one's attitude, behavior, and interaction with others. Regardless of its nature, whether exotic (not in the indigenous or locality before) or indigenous, religion is always accompanied by different norms, ***beliefs****, and* ***virtues*** *which must be abode by to increase the discipline, faith, and devotion to that particular religion or belief. We are not discussing a particular religion, whether monotheistic or polytheistic, but rather, we are looking at religion, regardless of its form, as an* ***etiquette of life****. Religion and beliefs provide us mortals (Humans) a framework on how we should behave and interact with others of the same faith and beliefs (Religion) or different ones. Many religions teach their followers to treat others with kindness, respect, and compassion, which are part of humanity's*

natural laws. These help us understand how we react to friends, family, and strangers. Religious beliefs instil strong faith and determination into one's life, which allows one to develop strong personal values like honesty, integrity, and generosity. With these serving as a foundation in the person's life, they can make informed decisions for both their lives and others.

Many of us have heard stories where people are cast out of their families or communities due to the breakage of specific values of a religion, belief, or even a tradition. The main reason for this can be understood by knowing the impact the beliefs, religion, or tradition has imposed on the people in that particular community; we all have free will and the ability to make decisions for our lives once we attain the age of maturity however, the norms, beliefs, and traditions that we got nurtured from our childhood help us groom well. The ability of any religion or belief to propagate from generation to generation is observed in the positive impact on the society in which it is being practiced. Religion and beliefs avail us with a sense of ***community*** *and* ***belonging****. For example, one of the monotheistic religions (****Islam****) has a saying: "****A Muslim is a brother to another Muslim****." This brotherhood they talk about is much stronger than blood brotherhood; thus, if one is born Muslim or a convert, that person's brotherhood connection to* *his religious brothers is far more strong than from their blood brothers. In simple ways, brotherhood in this belief, is priotised based on belief and religious aspects than blood connection. Even in many other monotheistic religions and polytheistic religions, they have values that give them a sense of belonging.*

A lot more lies in the similarities and togetherness brought about by the religion or belief regarding worship, celebrations, and support for one another. This creates a sense of ***connectedness*** *among people of the same religion or belief, allowing them to express their sense of purpose, which might seem hard to find elsewhere. The different systems portrayed by different beliefs and religions give them unique etiquettes that help* ***bind people*** *of that belief or religion and help them not to go astray. The practices such as* ***prayer, fasting, attending religious services, giving charity,*** *and* ***following specific dietary restrictions*** *help maintain the people on the path as designed by their belief or religion. Some religions, such as Christianity, Islam, Buddhism, Hinduism, and many others, have different prayer times, which range from daily, weekly, and even annually, such as daily five times prayer for Muslims, weekly church services for many Christian faiths, annual celebrations such as* ***Eid-prayers, Christmas, Easters, Pongal, Holi,*** *and many others. These all help the individuals to connect* *with their spirituality and feel peace and calm. I remember when I was in India for my studies; I saw my friends show massive respect to religious leaders and religious monasteries such as temples, mosques, and churches.*

*Some of my Hindu friends used to kneel, prostrate and even bow every time we passed a temple or a picture of one of their gods. The point is not to show religious extremism, but one saying goes, "**The fear of the Lord is the beginning of wisdom.**" And we all need wisdom and other things. Some activities such as fasting, which are very common in many religions, especially Islam, Christianity, Buddhism, and Hinduism, which involve abstaining from food, specific activities, and water for a specified period of time, help people to demonstrate their level of devotion, faith, and discipline which at a certain point can serve as a reminder to the blessings one has in their lives. Religious services and activities help us interact, understand our worth and purpose and practice charitable activities; hence, engaging in one or two religious activities is always essential. These activities create a robust sense of community and belonging in one's life; services such as singing hymns, reciting prayers, participating in communion, religious tours, community charity, and marriage ceremonies are significant in one's life as they uplift and create a meaningful feature in one's life and the* *community.*

Moral and ethical values are hugely dependent on the faith of an individual. I wanted to exchange money from one currency to another; I had tried forex, but all those I went to claimed not to exchange my country's currency, and I wondered why? Was it because my currency was not money, or was it so low that it was not worth exchanging? Anyways, all that puzzled me, and I left it; hence I decided to go to the bank with the hope that, maybe since forex businesses are small-scale, they feared exchanging as they might get losses. So I headed into a bank and tried to explain what I wanted, and I was headed to the forex section, the story repeated. Many religions teach compassion, forgiveness, humility, and selflessness, which are critical factors in guiding people through life challenges and how they interact with others. At the bank, I was chased; I was then hopeless. A golden rule in almost all religions states, " ***Treat others how you would like to be treated****." And this keeps many religious and belief-grained people to be humble, respectful, and calm with others regardless of the situation. The principle promotes empathy, kindness, and respect for others; hence it is a guiding force for treating people in every place, be it home, workplace, school, and others, regardless of their differences, be it background or culture.*

Before I left the bank, I requested to see the manager because my home account had money, but I didn't know how to make a transaction, and it was getting late. Being that I was in a foreign land and they never knew how much I had in my pockets, they immediately allowed me to see the manager, and as we talked, I saw a holy book which I was very versed with. I diverted my conversation to the book, and he told me about his only son converting to a religion he never believed, and then because he was a person who respected all religions and faiths, the book was given to him by his son. He kept it on his office shelf, where he kept religious books. Cutting everything short, the man decided to help me with the amount I needed, and he further gave me a night at his house in his guest lounges. Many religious aspects include forgiveness, both seeking and offering to those who have wronged. Negative energy and emotions are driven and amplified by grudges and hatred we store or portray to others. This reduces our productivity and beauty of both the heart and the tongue, making us rude, jealous, and envious. This phenomenon exacerbates the desire to commit sin and bad acts to others and ourselves. Many reports of suicide and murder have been induced due to jealousy, anger, envy, and deeply hidden grudges against people with no hope of forgiving and forgetting.

Imagine when you have a good job with proud bosses and workmates, and suddenly one of the bosses echoes out something that tarnishes your name in front of other workmates; the next day, the desire to work in the same company decreases, and the anger and jealous on that boss increases, and every time you see them, your productivity decreases making you a bad employee. However, you or the boss might be having a problem no one knows, and the only way to find out is by seeking forgiveness and breaking down to understand why they would want to tarnish your name. Such incidences are common in families, businesses, and even schools; however, they sometimes test our faith, resistivity, and resilience. Once we fail, they take away our power to seek forgiveness and always make us rude, angry, and angry negative. Most religions and beliefs' biggest challenge is the desire to extract and milk people of their materials, making these places never safe and welcoming for most people. However, teachings such as serving others, practicing humility, and encouraging individuals to put the needs of others first than their own in building the greater good are sources of morals, love, and helping each other. When people practice such religious morals in their lives, they get a powerful insight and desire to promote social justice, equality, and charity because these principles guide people to take action to help others who are marginalized or oppressed.

Besides providing a sense of community and belonging for particular individuals of similar beliefs and religions, they are important to converge and nurture people affected by different life-threatening situations that make them feel isolated, disconnected, or even traumatized in society. In many incidences, people have testified to having obtained their connections, networks, and specific opportunities from their religious communities. Study groups, worship services, social events, and volunteer activities have provided a sense of camaraderie and shared purpose as people get together, work together, and all work towards achieving a common goal. Different belief domains have support programs for those disciples who are in difficult times and crises. Considering the recent Turkey earthquake, where millions of people were left homeless, many charity and rescue organizations of different religious domains were seen to provide help in any form to the affected individuals. When people are in difficult times, such as illnesses, loss, or financial struggles, some religious cults are designated to help such people. This helps with emotional and practical support, giving them a sense of comfort.

I was told a story by a friend who once used to work in a cemetery that one day he was tasked to clean the graves as the next day, a very important person in their community was to be buried. He started cleaning, but because the graves were very many and he was working alone, he cleaned till late evening. And as he was about to finish cleaning, he decided to rest a bit by placing his head on one of the gravestones. As he slumbered, he had a vision in his sleep when he was at the same place, and all the people from the graves were sitting with him and asking him questions as he answered. Someone from the dead then asked him why he did not believe in supreme creation, and his answers were vague, and he stuttered as he answered. Many of them then told him they were not ready to see a person who cleans them every day waste that goodness and then end up denied heaven. As he was trying to convince them, they all looked in one direction and paved the way for someone, he saw a man whom he had never recognized by face, and as he approached nearer, he heard a very loud voice calling him to wake up as the cemetery was to be closed. He never stayed the same from that day, and he kept asking himself questions and couldn't answer them. He once went to the church and met a priest who made sense of his dream and told him that he was very lucky the dead spoke to him and never caused harm to him, and as they were trying to trap his soul, an angel came to his rescue. We can't finish that story as it is not story time and even the person who narrated it to us was a priest who I think was trying to strengthen our beiliefs, however it was known in all our community that he was once a graves cleaner.

As humans, we all need to have the motive to do something, and records have it that in this century, the most motive for many people in the world comes from religious communities. Many religions have motivative figures in their beliefs which they take to be perfect and holy, such as prophets and saints for many monotheistic religions, gods, and goddesses for many polytheistic religions, and these have been for many years conferred as sources of inspiration and motivation for people in those religions. So many Christians get their motivation and inspiration from many Saints and people such as Mother Teresa, Saint Christiana, and Emil Zatopek; Muslims get more inspiration from their prophets, most importantly Muhammad (PBUH) and Caliphs (Abubakar, Umar, and others), while other polytheistic religions such as Hinduism get inspiration from Lord Krishna, Buddha, and others. Besides having a good connection in their life with religion or beliefs, one has to consider that these are the major leading cause of conflicts and division among different groups of people. The world witnessed a lot when many people use religion to justify the harmful and discriminatory actions they commit in society. Recognizing and respecting diversity among people in a given population is always important. Everyone must at least have one particular religion or belief they hold onto. Still, not everyone will have yours; understanding that people have different tastes and opinions is key to tolerance and compassion.

THREE

PERSONAL GROWTH

Personal growth literally has no absolute definition, but there are many ways in which it can be expressed when it comes to writing. Many elites and educators consider personal growth to be a series of continuous ***self-improvement*** *and* ***self-development*** *that aid in achieving an individual's full potential or the best version of oneself. It is a lot more than considering personal success. Still, it involves focusing more on the areas in one's life that they consider needing improvements and taking the required action and energy to bring about positive change in one's life. There are many forms of personal development, such as physical and health, knowledge and skills, development of new habits and behaviors, cultivating a positive mindset, and developing self-care and self-love. Many people consider taking two* *forms at a time while others consider one; depending on what your intuition is and what you think your better version is, the power lies within you as a person. We have witnessed many people investing millions in physical health to ensure they are their best versions. Many people get gym memberships to attain the type of body structure and posture they need. Its quite easy to notice that personal growth has a very huge impact to our life and personality in both society and communities we live in.*

In this century, where knowledge and skills are ***paramount****, and those who have information and cannot contemplate being useful have less value, many people have embarked on a journey to expand their knowledge and skills in different fields such as IT, Biology, Engineering, etc. Physics, and others. Exploring new possibilities and taking up new challenges in life help many people push themselves outside of their comfort zones and allow them to build their new versions leading to better achievements and growth. However, the desire for everyone to have good personal growth lies in the aspect of self-awareness, which allows individuals to understand their strengths and weaknesses and set measurable and time-bound goals. This process involves the person considering all the values, beliefs, and attitudes that govern them and analyzing the best ways in which all can be balanced. By developing a better understanding* *of themselves, they can identify their areas of improvement and set goals for personal growth. Imagine a person who is having restrictive health. Maybe they have a disease such as leukemia or any other terrible disease, and they think the best version of themselves is* ***Mohammed Ali****. Considering their weakness and strengths, this goal is time-bound and measurable, but it's not systematic and attainable; hence the different ethical conditions, values, and rules which govern their health and body can not allow them to have that personal growth strategy.*

*Hence, knowing their weakness and strengths allows them to understand where they can persist and how long they can persevere. The saying goes, "****When the going gets tougher, you harden and strengthen because storms can only last a few hours, but the results might be for years.****" Personal growth, on the other hand, requires a lot of commitment and devotion because sometimes we set goals that seem to be easily achieved in months or years but due to our lack of consistency, we might end up leaving them or even die without achieving any. When one gets committed to ongoing learning or transformation and self-reflection, one must know that taking responsibility for their development and actively seeking out opportunities for growth and development is their sole responsibility. One can use different* *strategies to set up a personal growth scheme for themselves and be sure to follow it for better results. Goal setting; The first stage in executing any plan is setting up a target goal; it involves identifying and defining specific areas in their life, allowing them to have a clear roadmap for achieving a desired outcome. However, a clear goal must be set, and it should be feasible and attainable. Imagine a skinny boy who signs up for a gym membership with the goal of achieving The Rock's (**Dwayne Johnson**) in a few months.*

*The goal is attainable but not feasible in a sense; building all the muscles and energy in a few months is hypothetical. Many analysis theorems have different analogies for goal setting, but the one I like most is the **SMART** goal-setting system. It informs of setting a goal that falls in the five systems of **Specific** meaning it should not be overlapping and non-directional to ensure that one can follow it with precision and commitment. **Measurable** to help one analyze the progress and understand how their intensity and energy went, this allows many people to increase their courage and enthusiasm towards doing something. **Achievable** or attainable to help one have a mindset of satisfaction and content that the set goal can be done and has ever been done thus it is not as extraordinary and hard as they think or perceive. **Relevant** or realistic because* *sometimes people set goals that cannot hold in their potential and they end up losing the morale of doing what they can do thinking they are good for nothing; thus when setting a goal it should be realistic for example if one is very good at solving challenging puzzles and mind games, they can set a goal to win the regional chess competition and if one is good at creating new ideas from scratch they can set a goal of winning an ideation pitching competition.*

***Time-bound** as a set goal might require much time than the individual can offer or even the time frame in which they set the goal to be achieved might be less or even more hence setting a good time for working on a certain goal is important because most skills and knowledge consume a lot of time and they require consistency. One can set a goal of winning the district marathon competition and decide to plan running for 1 hour three times per week which is an idea and fits into the time but one can also set a goal of participating in the Google codding competition but set a coding practice time of less than 30 minutes per day which of those do you think is a goal that is time-bound?*

***Cultivating self-awareness:** Humans are from the same genera and same species, but we have a lot more differences amongst ourselves even* *though we are from the same family and parents. The ability of a person to understand and recognize their thoughts and govern them to prevent them from quick decision-making and bad feelings, behavior, and unethical acts is the strongest challenge in personal growth. A lot of times, we see, hear, or even eyewitness situations where people fail to control their emotions, feelings, and even behavior, allowing them to influence their decision-making and end up making mistakes that can cost them a lifetime career or goal. Many people of great minds talked about how fast things get destroyed yet they took decades and decades to be built and furnished. It is always important to cultivate the highest level of your self-awareness as this can help you in identifying areas in your life where you need improvement, and it also helps you to set up strategies to make a plan of action towards improving them so that your actions can have a positive impact to you and others in society. Many ways have been taught and others encouraged by therapists but some of the best ways are through prayers, meditation, journaling, and seeking feedback from loyal people.*

Continuous learning: *The fact that people often look for the best of themselves and also what is considered better in the world at a certain time calls for continuous learning and gaining of skills. This allows improvement of existing* *skills and attaining new skills plus knowledge which at some point might seem so useful in a certain community. This step is crucial in personal development as it helps one to keep updated with the latest and advanced information, technology, and skills in a specific field of expertise. People develop reading cultures such as new books every month or two months and others engage in attending workshops, online courses, coding, and other skills.*

Practicing self-care: *allows a person to understand their health in terms of emotional, physical, and mental terms and find ways in which they can maintain its integrity and prevent it from facing threatening situations. The process involves activities such as medical checks, physical exercise, healthy eating, and others which aid in the reduction of stress, an increase in happiness and well-being, and an improvement in quality of life. Many people neglect their health and claim to be focused on developing skills and working so hard yet the body that allows them to do all the things they do is lacking. When it comes to self-care, also spiritual life helps to maintain the emotional aspects of one's health and therefore one has to pay attention to their connection with God or their beliefs. For IT and other professions whose schedule makes them work many hours and get less sleep, it is better to have time and get* *enough rest and let the body and mind relax because sometimes our body needs a reset from the stress encountered in the previous sessions and we just end up depriving that reset of it.*

Lastly, we can talk about embracing challenges; as we step out of our comfort zone, we face challenges, and these help us to think outside and beyond the box limits which makes us the ability to look at different perspectives of challenges. Different views of a problem give different solutions and whichever solution works best for us is always the right way to tackle a challenge. Our comfort zone always gives us content that we know enough, and we need not do anything more however, every time we step out of it, new challenges set into play and this gives us the ability to develop new skills and abilities which can increase our productivity. This also means making lots of mistakes and the best way is to learn from them but not have regret, as our mental health needs to be clear for us to be more productive. The more mistakes and failures, the more we learn and find different routes toward doing something. Resilience and persistency, in turn, make us yield. Challenges such as travel, public speaking, foreign countries, learning new languages, and others all are set to make our new versions. Enough for the pep talk, we can dive deep into the four most sacred and often non-spoken-about principles and etiquettes of personal development.

Gratitude

Remember that anyone (friends or family members) who always had beauty to show how appreciative and thankful they were once anything good or any help has been granted to them; I know you have one in mind and so does anyone. That person portrayed what is known as ***gratitude****. By dictionary definition, a person blesses with the gift of gratitude has the ability and passion to show a strong feeling of appreciation, thankfulness, and return of kindness to someone or something for what they have done to help them. This aspect is powerful when it comes to personal development and plays a vital role in enhancing one's life and etiquette. It involves* ***acknowledging*** *and* ***appreciating*** *the positive aspects of life both big and small and expressing a thankful heart for them. A lot of people consider this kind of portrayal a gift and others consider it as a personal nurture but in this case, we will consider it as a nurture. People grow up in different places which they call home whether with family or without. Learning how to be thankful and appreciative to anyone or something that has granted you help or any goodness is part of one's nurture. We are all not born with the attitudes, behavior, and norms we have but where we grow up and the society we live in impacts a lot from what we will portray* *to others.*

Practicing something regularly can lead to numerous benefits in both positive and negative ways such as improved mental well-being, stronger relationships, addictions, increased happiness, and increased depression; thus if one can develop a good strategic plan for practicing gratitude in their life, they can have a lot of benefits in life. When it comes to personal development, gratitude serves as a catalyst for self-improvement by shifting our focus from what we lack in life to what we have thus fostering a positive mindset. I know all of us in life have been in a situation where we needed to be like other people. I remember in my primary education, I was in a poor government school, and being hungry was a norm, and complaining about it was never raising any attention to anyone both at home and school. We could always leave home early in the morning at 6 AM, after fetching jerrycans of water from the well which was about 30 minutes' walk and we had to spend a day at school minus breakfast, and lunch. We admired our neighbors' children who were in good schools, had school vans pick them up, and had breakfast and lunch boxes packed.

Living in an extended family taught me a lot more than I could learn from any other place.

Every time we were trekking from school, we passed a vending kiosk for a woman whose name we even never knew till now, she always sold fruits. She cut the sugarcane stems for sale and she had the left upper seedling stem she could throw across the roadside every time we were from school we passed through that place and picked those seedlings and juice them out and quench our thirst as well as reduce the hunger because they contained sugar. Grandmother always cooked food in the evening that was if we left water fetched in the morning and we only had one meal in the home for more than five years, however, every time we had a meal our grandmother always emphasized being thankful and prayerful to God so that He can add more. After a while, one day we passed through the kiosk again and we saw good sugarcanes being thrown at the exact place we always picked the seedlings, we could not believe and we never took them because there were rampant cases of poisoning and kidnapping. The following day when we passed there the lady called us and gave us good sugarcane and she requested us to always come to her kiosk and ask for the sugarcane she was to give us for free.

I don't want to say that the story above might make sense to you about gratitude, but one day as we grew older and went back to our grandmother's place, we reminded ourselves of that time, and all of us deep in our hearts we could always pray for that lady to never fall sick and be healthy and gain more from what she does such that she could get more sugarcanes and we could get more seedlings to eat while we were from school. We prayed all that every time our grandmother told us to thank God after every meal, and prayer. By recognizing the good in our lives, we cultivate a sense of contentment and satisfaction which contributes to higher levels of self-esteem, self-content, and confidence. When we reflect on our experiences and learn from them it increases our ability to promote growth and resilience clearly understanding that situations are temporary thus at certain a time a breakthrough can come. Gratitude is essential in building and maintaining healthy relationships with others, through respect, kindness, and appreciation for their actions, support, and contributions in your life. By expressing gratitude, we acknowledge the efforts and thoughtfulness of others which leads to strengthening the bonds we share with them.

Every time we express high levels of gratitude to others, we create a stronger sense of connection, empathy, and reciprocity which facilitates the development of a positive social environment. One may ask themselves the ways in which they can express gratitude and the answer is simple. Can you show someone that you are appreciative of their help and if yes, you need not go to school to learn this? Different forms of expression happen which can be verbal, writing, journaling and even engaging in acts of kindness. Some religions and beliefs take it to the next level and tell their believers to show appreciation even when there is help granted by anyone and this is because this type of gratitude is restricted to spiritual appreciation of God's blessings. Thanking God because of the gift of life, fitness, and a roof over one's head is also gratitude. To cultivate this type of mindset one needs to be consciously shifting their perspective to focus on the positives even during challenging times and difficulties. This does not mean that one should work tooth and nail to suppress the negative emotions but rather find a way of acknowledging and learning from them while recognizing the good that exists that that particular moment. Let's now embark on a journey to develop and incorporate gratitude in our personal development and etiquette. Try doing the following in your daily life:

***Develop a gratitude journal**: this gives you a good reflection of the things that took place during each day and screen out those you have to be grateful for by considering their **positivity, kindness**, and **blessings** to you. Setting aside a few minutes of each day to write down a few things you are grateful for. You can write down literally everything from simple pleasures, achievements, and moments of joy to acts of kindness you experienced. Every time you sit* *back and reflect on the good things you did or that happened to you during the day, it encourages you to increase the growth of your seed of gratitude. Imagine a place where everyone has only one perfectly functioning organ sense like sight, taste, smell, touch, and hearing. In this scenario, everyone will be dependent on the other and not fall into a pit hole, not take too salty foods, not get burnt by fire, not eat awful-smelling things, and others. The people in this society will all be grateful for each other, and this allows the continuity of this system. When you write down the gifts, and blessings you had during the day, you help yourself to increase your cultivation of the attitude of gratitude.*

***Express appreciation**: through simple "**thank you**" or heartfelt note allows people to know that you value their presence and actions in your life. Do not hesitate to express thanks to God and others. From those around you such as family, friends, and workmates, take time and show them that you are grateful and thankful for their efforts in your life. It's better to be true to yourself and **genuinely** say "thank you" specifically **acknowledging** and **appreciating** others for their actions and effort in your life. Picking up your phone from your table, or pocket and call your children, family member, or friend and thank them for being a blessing in your life. This will allow people in your life* *to understand their position and relevance to you. However, it will instill in you the gift of appreciation for others and their actions or support in your life. Practice mindfulness: staying aware and present of the positive and beautiful moments that occur in one's life is paramount to having gratitude. Being mindful of the beauty around you, the kindness of others to you and other people and the opportunities that come your way allows us to reflect on how blessed and lucky we are; this makes us appreciative of both God and those that laid their hands on us to make it where we are in life. Many people go out in the wild and focus on the beauty of nature and its coexistence, savor the taste of the foods and others appreciate the warmth of the sun on their skin which gives them the ability and courage to always be thankful to God for the limitless blessings they receive from Him without return. Being fully present and attentive gets one to appreciate and recognize small blessings and gifts that often go unnoticed.*

Share acts of kindness**: small gestures such as lending a helping hand, offering words of encouragement, and listening to other people express their views help one to develop and extend gratitude. One should always look at opportunities that allow them to help, support or uplift someone's day making it fruitful and memorable. Even when it's a simple offering of* *a* ***listening ear, volunteering your time *for a cause you care about, or even surprising someone you care bout with a small thoughtful gesture or gift. These small things help build a bridge of kindness and beauty within you as a person and the person whom you showed the actions to allowing you both to enhance your sense of gratitude and fulfillment. A lot of people think that kindness and helping are material but often people need simple gestures and shoulders to lie on and feel loved, protected, and appreciated.****Reflect on the challenges****: finding lessons and silver linings in situations of difficulty allows one to reflect on their personal growth and strengthen them to increase their potential to overcome obstacles. Taking challenges that one faces being learning moments is a good way to deal with all the negativity that might come with them, and this allows one to understand that everything comes for a season and eventually seasons come to pass. Being complaints every time you get a challenge limits your ability to grow and reason maturely thus it deprives you of one's ability to develop problem-solving skills and decision-making skills in life. If one makes an effort of finding lessons and positive vibes within the difficult experiences they pass through, they must be able to evaluate their personal growth and resilience allowing them to build a robust level of gratitude. Actually, by also reframing challenges as opportunities for growth and development in one's life, one can develop a* *mindset that appreciated both ups and downs in life and this allows them to understand how life is fair and just. We can try a lot of things to build a strong robust level of gratitude, but we all have to remember that, gratitude is not what we read or see and go away. It is practice and this requires consistency and intention.*

Kindness.

*The ability of someone to be **helpful, generous**, and **caring about others** regardless of their nature and background is what is known as **kindness**. This property is a fundamental virtue and greatly enhances the interactions of that person with others thus creating stronger relationships. When one makes this essential in their lives, it goes beyond the simple act of being polite and encompasses compassion, empathy, and genuine concern for the well-being of others. From different perspectives, kindness can be understood as a **vital component** of social interaction, relationships, and the overall fabric of the society in which one lives. Families, cultures, and nations are being bound together due to the kindness each person portrays to the other. It creates a crucial role in creating and maintaining social bonds within communities and through different acts of kindness by the people in a given community, the development of trust, cooperation, and reciprocity among people is achieved. Acts such as helping hands, caring hearts, and loving each other in communities enable the establishment of a sense of connectedness and strengthen the social fabric of the community.*

Many norms, beliefs, and religions influence kindness both positively and negatively, however, the majority of these norms or beliefs encourage their people to spread kindness and love for everyone whether insiders or outsiders and they furthermore nurture the people in the community to promote socialism and equality amongst others so that ***discrimination*** *and* ***marginalization*** *are not experienced in that community. Different societies or communities define kindness differently and this is done by the establishment of certain standards of behavior that define what is considered kind and appropriate. Some communities may consider giving a token to beggars on the streets as a kindness because one is trying to help a person in need and most times those who are begging on the streets are disabled people however in some communities this act might be seen as promotion of bad morals in society and hence it's not considered to be an act of kindness. The simple reason is that in the world of today, disability is not inability hence people who often beg on the streets are lazy and do not what to work with their hands to earn a living but rather consider being given.*

This comes to conclusion when people who are more disabled than those begging on the streets are running businesses and can support their life with the little, they obtain from the business while in some cases people fake being disabled so that they can get free materials, sympathy, target people for robbery and even some go be rude, impolite and illy nurtured. Above all the norms and principles set by the different beliefs, and religions, become a guiding standard for giving help and showing kindness to others hence these acts are seen as normative behavior that is valued and encouraged in society. Kindness can be natural as most of us know intuitively that when one is hurt, we can't hurt them more, we need to show them care and kindness or even when someone is ill, we show them care, love, pray for them and even be kind to them so that they can get well. These and many other forms of kindness are natural and require no learning however, learned kindness is also needed and this is obtained from society and surrounding. Kindness is learned and reinforced through socialization, from a young age people socialize through their families, school, friends, and communities and this helps them to understand the importance of showing care, love, and being kind to others.

This process involves observations, instructions, and reinforcement which enables the individuals to acquire the knowledge and skills necessary to engage in kind behavior. Imagine a trip camp into the wild, if people are grouped into different groups without bias selection, the probability that people who have grudges against each other are in the same group is half, hence if the group is instructed to accomplish certain tasks, the chances of failures in the first trials will be high but as people get to socialize better, understand each other, respect each other and their decisions, the chances of success in the proceeding trials are high. The simple explanation is, being kind to someone regardless of their acts and what they did to you does cause a positive energy flow and can end up creating a new stronger relationship. Showing people kindness has a duo direct impact on the individuals' well-being and overall quality of life. Acts such as providing emotional support, offering help during times of need, showing empathy, and contributing to the formation of social support networks and others serve as an important sources of emotional, instrumental, and information support which enhances people's resilience and satisfaction in their social life. This effect happens for both the individual showing kindness to others and to those to whom kindness is being offered. Here are some of the ways in which kindness can be an etiquette of one's life thorugh practice:

Consider portraying respect to others and yourself**: Kindness always starts with respecting the inherent worth and dignity of everyone in a community including yourself. This involves treating others with courtesy, politeness, and fairness regardless of their nature and background. Above all, one needs* *to be considerate and kind to themselves so as to increase their motive and strength to keep going. Considering the feelings, needs, and rights of others, helps to create an environment where everyone feels valued, safe, and included. Many scenarios where people who are neglected, disrespected, and considered insignificant in society end up adopting non-ethical or immoral behaviors and activities such as heavy alcoholism, rape, drugs, and suicide. Because everything starts with "**you**" as an individual, then your self-respect and consideration are vital for advancing and promoting the ability to give kindness to others.* ***Keeping one's emotional and psychological health fit, t*his is one of the most required fitness for anyone who intends to give kindness to anyone this is because most kindness needed by people is more emotional than material hence having strong emotional and psychological health is important.*

Having empathy and understanding: *One must have the ability to acknowledge and accept to understand and share the feeling of another person in different ways which can include active listening, and comprehension of the struggles and joys of the other person. If one fails to cultivate empathy, one can not relate or step into the shoes of the person's experience in order to comprehend and realize the pain or joy and pleasure someone is passing or has* *passed through and this can limit their ability to be kind and give a helping hand. There are some people who observe others passing through a given situation and just because they have ever had a similar situation, they can comprehend and end up giving help and showing kindness, however, there are those others who have ever passed through the same situation but their phase was short-lived because situations can be similar but not the same for everyone. These people might feel less empathetic and less likely to be kind to the sufferer at the moment. Empathetic understanding allows people to respond with compassion, support, and encouragement to those passing through a given situation.*

Practice thoughtful gestures: *Actions and small acts that promote kindness instill a profound impact on the individuals and the community we live in. Simple acts such as a genuine smile, a greeting, holding the door for someone, and offering assistance to those in need can generate a lot of positivity and enlightenment in one's life and brighten one's day. These guests demonstrate care, love, respect, and consideration for others in the community making people feel acknowledged and appreciated. Saying "**good morning**" to a colleague at work or even to a toddler you meet on the way to college doesn't reduce the value or titles you have but rather creates a positive* *energy and connection between people and the community. At times these small acts of kindness are the ones that make people understand our importance in society and others get to feel cared for. Imagine if someone was greeting you every day you passed by them as you head to work for the past three years, and one day you never get a greeting from them anymore? The effect of missing a greeting from that person will be so intense that one will have to make a follow-up so as to understand what happened to that person.*

Forgiveness

One's ability ***to let go of past grievances*** *and the* ***strength to have positive understanding*** *and* ***compassion*** *for anyone describes the level of one's forgiving personality. This etiquette is unique from others that we will encounter in this book because it is a transformative virtue and allows someone to heal deeply, grow physically and mentally and maintain harmonious relationships with others in society or community. This act which seems hard and life-taking to many is not only a noble act but also a powerful tool for personal growth and emotional well-being. A lot of times like in my village or even other communities we witness people claiming that they will never forgive someone in their life, and some take it a step further to lament and curse them from attending their burial. For some communities, this might mean nothing but, in my community, when one doesn't attend your burial, it's more of a big deal than one not attending your wedding. Different communities have a different respect for the dead and most communities believe that those who never attend the burial of the person in the community are haunted by their souls which I can't say is true or false but it's a big deal for some communities, hence if one lament and vows that you never step on their burial, it's* *one of the last things one needs to hear in my community.*

In our journey through life, we inevitably encounter situations in which we as people feel wronged, betrayed, disappointed, disrespected, or even hurt by others; this is normal for everyone in this world. These experiences leave deep physical and emotional scars in our life and some harbor resentment within us. The most challenging part is holding to these grudges too tightly that we fail to let go of them hence carrying them everywhere, and forward in our future which continues to propagate negativity and prevents us from moving forward. Yes by embracing forgiveness, we can break free off from the chains of these ***deep scars, anger,*** *and* ***resentment*** *allowing us to open ourselves to healing, peace, freedom, and positive change in our lives. By the way, forgiveness is not limited to others, it also includes forgiving ourselves and this normally happens when one keeps holding onto self-guilt, self-blame, and regret for past mistakes or shortcomings instead of treating them as lessons and learning from them. Many people have the ability to forgive others no matter what the mistake, damage, or hurt they have caused in their life, but they often get a hard time and challenging notions when it comes to forgiving themselves which keeps them trapped in their past mistakes and these dwell into them* *preventing their personal development and growth.*

***Self-forgiveness** is crucial and a key role in the path to personal growth and self-compassion which boost one's magnitude to personal development. The ability to recognize and understand one's fallibility and embrace self-forgiveness plays a major role in learning, decision making, and the development of empathy which paves the way for one to obtain lessons from their mistakes and strive towards becoming better versions of themselves. As we noted earlier, this is not something one must read in a book and gain knowledge but rather it is a skill that must be put into practice and this allows one to cultivate empathy and understanding of the fact that people are prone to errors and that is what makes us humans as these errors allow us to keep learning. People have differences in perspectives; we are all liable to make errors but the best among us is the one who has a broader understanding and acknowledgment of the mistakes through forgiveness and extending empathy and compassion to others. Forgiving doesn't mean the past is forgotten, but rather when we forgive, **we choose to focus on building a better future** based on understanding and empathy. In most cases, people focus on the past which doesn't even exist anymore, and neglect the present which has a significant effect on the future, and* *this makes people lack focus and vision.*

As we are all humans, we know that forgiving is not easy, and developing this forgiving personality is not a piece of cake thus we need time and effort to fully let go of the hurt and resentment. This journey is hard but it's a worthwhile endeavor for the sake of one's well-being and the betterment of one's relationship with themselves and others in the community. When one forgives, they learn from the past and this allows them to foster healthier connections with other people, promoting trust among others, development of empathy for themselves and others, and creating a circle of people filled with mutual respect and love. In this way, one gets emotional liberation and personal transformation. Many people claim that some acts or things done to them, and those they did as well can't be forgiven and this is really sad and heart-breaking because ***someone accepts and sacrifices themselves to imprison themselves in their pas****t inhibiting personal growth and development. I can not stand to say they are wrong, or they are right however, finding a way to forgive and let go of the past is much better and gives more relief and freedom in one's life. Developing a forgiving personality requires self-reflection, empathy, and commitment to personal growth and the good news is that we are giving our readers some of the things one can incorporate in their life to* *cultivate a forgiving personality:*

Develop self-awareness: *one must begin by recognizing their own emotions and the impact of holding onto grudges in their life. This will help them increase their level of self-respect and understanding. If one gets to know that forgiveness is not a weakness but a courageous choice to encourage emotional liberation, it will help them to increase their ability to acknowledge mistakes, obtain lessons from them, and let go of the past focusing on the future.*

Cultivation of empathy and perspective-taking: *This works better when someone puts themselves in one's shoes and tries to understand their motivations, experiences, and struggles hence one can develop sympathy and allows them to see the humanity in others which makes forgiving easier. We all know we humans make mistakes and regardless of one's status, the mistakes we make are always hurting both us and others thus judging so quickly is never the solution to many things. Just as it is important and useful to forgive others, it is equally important to forgive oneself. One has to understand and accept deep in their hearts that making mistakes is part of being human and they further have to embrace self-compassion. This involves treating oneself with kindness and* *understanding.*

Letting go of the resentment: *A lot of times people don't accept or acknowledge the pain caused by the offense or mistake done to them or by them which keeps them trapped in their past mistakes thus if one lets go of this burden by making conscious decisions to release it out helps in development and growth. One must understand that holding a grudge or anger only prolongs ones suffering emotionally and physically preventing both mental and physical healing.*

Communicating and expressing emotions: *Everyone can give strong evidence about people being highly reserved and silent no matter what happened to them. This is to some people regarded as strength but in my opinion, communicating my feelings with the person who hurt me or any situation that caused me to get hurt both physically and emotionally is more ideal. One must try being honest and open to communicate with the person who hurt them or to anyone they trust about a situation that hurt them which can lead to resolution, mature understanding, and ultimately forgiveness or in the worst-case self-relief to prevent carrying the burden further. At times people find this difficult and the best way to go over it is to cultivate self-forgiveness so that one prevents being a prisoner* *of their past.*

Setting healthy boundaries: *Many people might take advantage of the fact that you forgive them to continue hurting you and this is known by almost everyone and it is one of the reasons why people don't want to forgive anymore. However, establishing clear boundaries that protect one's well-being and prevent future harm can be a solution. Everyone has their safe zone, and one has to set clear and healthy principles and boundaries they must adhere to prevent being taken for granted when they do forgive others. This ensures that one obtains self-respect and a healthy relationship after an act of forgiveness.*

Last but not least, one has to practice mindfulness and acceptance, seeking support when needed, continued forgiving, and embrace gratitude and positivity: One has to be aware of their thoughts and emotions allowing one to accept the past and focus on the present moments which heals them and moves them forward. In cases where deep betrayal or trauma a person must consider seeking support from friends, family, or professional therapy and counseling, however, forgiveness is not a one-time act but an ongoing practice to actively remind oneself of the benefits of forgiving which can allow them to integrate it in their lives as natural and effortless.

Self-Care

Nurturing and prioritizing one's own self physical, emotional, and mental well-being are essential in this evolving world and this is simply known as self-care. The process involves one understanding and developing a priority for taking care of themselves in order to maintain a balanced and fulfilling life. This concept got a negative perception from many critics and other people I may say, they considered this as a selfish nature however, self-care gives one the power and motivation to put into practice necessary routines that allow them to install and portray the best versions of themselves in all aspects of life. If one denies smoking a cigarette regardless of the conditions be it peer pressure or weather condition with reasons they take genuine for their health, emotion, and physical strength that person is portraying self-care. This doesn't necessarily mean that those who are doing the act are not, but this concept depends on the person because everyone knows their body, mind, and soul differently. One's ability to reject driving after drinking is self-care because when one is sober the accuracy of our decision-making increases than when intoxicated.

In this fast-paced world, many of us neglect our own needs and prioritize the needs of others (selfless) little do they know that self-care is essential in maintaining overall health and happiness for them and others around them. One has to set aside dedicated time and resources to recharge, rejuvenate and nurture themselves. Let's explore the types of self-care one needs to work on for better personal growth and development.

Physical self-care: *Our bodies are like machines highly compartmentalized with cells, organs, and systems which must have certain needs met for proper functioning. Attending to the body's needs such as rest, nutrition, exercise, and relaxation through practices such as enough sleep, eating nourishing meals, engaging in regular physical activities, and finding moments of calmness and relaxation. This boosts one's health and energy levels allowing enhanced productivity. I remember one time when I was in high school, our biology teacher on Tuesdays used to come in after the first lesson in the afternoon with chocolates in class and distributed them to us all. He then sat down as we chew them, and we jazzed with him for the first ten minutes before he could take the class. One day, I asked him the reason for the chocolates, and he told me to wait the next day. The next day after I asked, he never brought them and once he entered the class, he* *immediately started teaching and after the first ten minutes, we were all dozing and tired. He then called me in front of the class and asked me to explain what was happening in class. I tried explaining and he told me that he had answered the question I asked him the day before. One might ask how this scenario relates to physical self-care but in times of afternoon the body utilizes energy faster than it's supplied; mostly in our schools which are exhaustive, students lose concentration and only want the day to end so that they can relax however the teacher knew this and decided to always sacrifice ten minutes and chocolates to get our efforts rise up and alertness so as to save the remaining fifty minutes and make us understand what he was teaching.*

Emotional self-care: *The brain governs emotions, but the heart, face, and other emotion-sensitive organs express them hence one must acknowledge and honor their emotions. This involves a series of activities that can be physiological or mental such as allowing oneself to feel and process these emotions in their life without judging or suppressing them. Some emotions are hormonally controlled while most of the emotions we encounter regardless of gender are nervously controlled hence understanding them is critical to emotional self-care. Individuals must get involved in activities that bring joy, self-compassion, and support* *seeking from loved ones to cultivate maximum emotional self-care. Many times, people get heartbroken by loved ones, and in their reactions, they express violent emotions which creates fighting scenes and suicide which are uncalled for, however, there are a few who are very good at controlling their emotions and this helps them to pass through times which are tough and challenging in life. Having good emotional self-care enables people to build robust emotional resilience and maintain a healthy emotional balance in life.*

Mental self-care: *Let us not confuse emotional self-care and mental self-care, these two are completely different. While emotional focuses on one's response to emotional triggers such as nervous and hormonal interventions to enable a person to manage their reactions to incidents that bring emotions, mental self-care dives deeper to nurture and sharpen the mind (brain and soul) through different activities that stimulate the intellectual abilities and cultivate inner power of one's mind. Activities such as reading, learning new skills, solving puzzles, and engaging in activities that create pursuits can aid one develop a strong mental self-care routine. Many people have a routine of long time usage of technological devices such as mobile phones, television, and gaming consoles, laziness in learning new things and skills, and ignoring challenging modes which can boost* *ones thinking and creative development abilities; these lead to burnout and decrease one's mental clarity.*

Social self-care: *There is a saying that goes, "that birds of the same feathers, flock together" and so people of the same social system will always be together. One must understand that it is difficult to obtain the best level of self-care when one's social environment is not adhering to the change they are opting for. Social self-care involves setting up healthy relationships and boundaries in their social interactions which will help them to promote self-care. This can be done by changing people in one's circle and including or leaving people who are supportive and uplifting one another in terms of promoting healthy activities and the cultivation of positivity. While some people find the "me" time more useful in developing their social life allowing them to increase their introspection and personal growth. If one tries to nurture their connections, seek meaningful conversations, and participate in activities that bring them a sense of belonging in the community can help them to increase the magnitude of their social self-care routine.*

Spiritual self-care: *Everyone has that inner connection to the spiritual realm or called the abstract universe in which only our inner self* *can connect also known as the souls. People must understand that nourishment of one's spiritual connections depending on their beliefs and practices is one of the best ways to cultivate the highest level of self-care. Activities such as meditation, prayer, reading holy books such as the Bible, Quran, and others, listening to spiritual music, spending time in nature, and pursuing spiritual teachings from worshiping centers and shrines help people to foster a sense of purpose, meaning and connection with something greater than themselves. People must also know that self-care is not a one-size-fits-all approach thus it depends deeply on a personal journey with increased self-awareness and self-reflection. It encompasses understanding and honoring one's unique needs and finding practices that resonate with their preferences, beliefs, and values.*

FOUR

SOCIAL INTERACTIONS

*The verbal and non-verbal interactions or communications between us and other people in our circles or communities allow us to connect, understand and relate to each other. This is the reason for the famous saying that "**Humans are social beings**". Social interactions shape us and play a crucial role in our daily lives, the relationships we have and those we make hence our overall well-being. All these interactions are governed by a set of rules and norms called social etiquette which guide us in behavior through nurturing and relations with others in society. These norms or principles can be hugely categorized into four major sub-classes which include communication, listening, empathy, and respect. The principles help us to navigate various social contexts and maintain positive and respectful interactions with others around* *us. There are many activities that fit into this broad concept such as greetings, healthy and non-healthy conversations, gestures, body language, and other forms of information exchange. Social interactions are not meant to be only healthy ones but rather they depend on the type of relationships we have with others in a community.*

Greetings to one another in a social network is common as people in each social network tend to have healthy social interaction. Body gestures such as a handshake, smiling, holding hands and many others might indicate healthy social interaction which in which respect, love, and care are involved whereas other gestures like tough eye contact might show signs of unhealthy social interaction which might call for fights or challenges (duos) amongst the individuals in each society. Socialization occurs at different levels in a community and in various settings like family gatherings, workplace environments, social events, and public spaces as well, these all involve elements of social interaction in which individuals associate and interact with each other. For effective social interaction to occur in a community, there have to be verbal and non-verbal skills like listening, empathy, clear communication, and appropriate body language. In most cases when a few of these skills are missing, interactions don't yield positive results thus people might end up fighting, disrespecting each other or even having torn relationships. However, the most common cause of these unhealthy social interactions in the community is a lack of clear communication and inappropriate body language.

In most African communities people often don't like finger-pointing them and also disrespect their loved ones like parents or family members and this can cause fights and continued hatred amongst people. Therefore, with proper etiquette (social manners), communities provide a framework for polite and considerate behavior for proper and healthy social interactions in communities and this is nurtured from home (family). This ensures that individuals are respectful, considerate, and sensitive to the needs and feelings of others allowing the creation of a positive and harmonious social environment for fostering healthy relationships. However, these norms, principles, or behaviors (some but not all) might vary depending on the region, countries, ethics, culture, and context where one lives or originates but there are those which are universally appreciated.

Being respectful and showing courtesy towards others in society as well as using polite language, maintaining eye contact, and giving others undivided attention when speaking instills a lot of social respect and healthy relationship in the community. Sometimes people just want someone to listen to them express their feelings and emotions (active listening), and this helps them to be understanding and considerate. Body language such as nodding and maintaining eye contact shows that one is concentrated and has undivided attention towards the conversation. While many people would want to talk about what is troubling them others might enjoy being silent which helps them to contemplate and have a clear picture of what is going on in their lives. One had to be mindful of personal space and maintain an appropriate physical distance, this is one form of respecting one's boundaries and use of open and friendly body language like smiling, open postures, and gestures. A lot of people get more sensitive as they age, and this makes them prone to noticing errors, disrespect, and even quick judgments due to reduced humor and funny moments. One needs to be empathetic toward others' feelings and perspectives, and this can be done by avoiding the use of offensive or judgemental remarks and being mindful of cultural differences, age, and affiliations.

Many people are so reactive when it comes to their religions, cultures, and ethnicities thus we must be cautious when joking or bluffing on matters that involve such issues. In this modernized world, almost everyone possesses a cell phone (smartphone) and nowadays emails are not through mail centers which usually took days and weeks to get hence they are instant on our devices. The issue of effective communication calls in hand punctuality and being responsive, a lot of people are fond of postponing urgent communications and giving less priority to people most especially those in their quick access such as family and work. Arriving on time for social engagements and having quick responses to invitations or messages saves people time, money, and resources. At some point, people consider reliability not by financial means or material gains but by the reaction time, frequency, and punctuality one has when it comes to situations of different types. Being reliable and respectful in nature demonstrates consideration and thoughtfulness to others in one's circle or community. On the same note, here comes another thing that has made life in this twenty-first century more disrespectful "Social media" and a lot of people have poor netiquettes which makes poor social media etiquette.

On media especially the most famous ones such as TikTok, Instagram, Twitter, and others, people have used bad language, expose nudes, deprived people of privacy, and others leading to poor social media engagement. One must be mindful of the language they use, what they post, the tone, the people who view and comment, respecting others' privacy, and engaging in meaningful and respectful discussions. Below are the four main social etiquettes that one must be keen on for effective and harmonious social interaction in society.

Communication

Personal and professional social interaction hugely depend on communication and this bases as the cornerstone of relationships as well. It involves the exchange of ideas, thoughts, and emotions which enable us individuals to connect, understand and collaborate with each other. As moral etiquette guides us through behavior for better ***socialization, communication*** *etiquette serves as a vital framework for fostering meaningful connections and avoiding misunderstandings with others in our communities. This lays a strong foundation for building and nurturing relationships through different activities such as listening, showing respect, and expressing genuine interest in others allowing us to create an environment conducive to trust and understanding. By doing so, we foster a strong connection with each other and enhance our quality of interaction and association. Almost 80% of people in the world use verbal communication and thus one has to take note of the following three key things:*

Clarity and brevity: *It is always better for one to be clear while communicating and make sure that precise explanations and discussions are put forward so that one can minimize the* *misunderstandings that could arise amongst people due to exhaustive discussions. Most people have a deeper understanding of words used in a conversation thus one needs to be so simple with the language and organize their thoughts coherently allowing them to express the ideas with precision. In most cases when one is talking to peers, they can use slang which might be of a different case when talking to family or coworkers and bosses. The choice of words and phrases matters a lot depending on who one is communicating to and how sensitive and strong the topic of discussion is.*

Tone and body language: *often times people get offended when we communicate with them just by them reading and processing our tone and body language hence it is necessary for one to pay attention to the tone of their voice and non-verbal cues while communicating. In most settings a loud and vibrant tone might be easily welcomed and better at delivering information in a crowd while it could be rude while talking with loved ones or peers. Shying away from one's eyes might symbolize being a liar more so if one is trying to persuade someone to do something while in some cases it might signify respect and deep affection for someone. One must maintain a positive and open posture while communicating and use appropriate words, phrases, and body language such as eye contact to have meaningful communication* *because these convey sincerity and engagement.*

Respect and Empathy: *People get uplifted by words and humiliated by words as well. One has to understand that while they are delivering communication, one had to be empathetic and respectful because words not only wow the ears of people but also affect their feelings. One must understand the different perspectives of their communication and lay boundaries to avoid conflicting and contradicting others in a harsh and disrespectful manner. This way one creates a safe and supportive environment where everyone listening to the communication feels valued. Sometimes people might insist to give negative responses and criticism but one must understand that before reacting to anything they have to be well acquainted with enough information or else one can call it pass.*

Not everyone will be focused on what one is speaking. Whenever there is communication, a few people will be focused on non-verbal communication such as ***body language,expressions****, and* ***gestures****. Nodding one's head during communication often symbolizes an understanding of what is being communicated, and most times communicators will portray a genuine and gentle smile to convey the message of warmth and friendliness. Practicing active listening and reading allows* *one to give full attention to the speaker or the author by maintaining eye contact and concentration which avoids one from getting distracted. People must also consider the mindful use of technology, in this evolving world, technology had become integral to communication and thus it is important to use it reasonably. We always get engaged in digital communication and be prompted to respond to messages, reactions, and votes. One must be cautious and mindful while doing so because improper use of words, grammar, caps, and others which may have a different interpretation by others must be keenly aware of as most people might consider them rude, humiliating, inhumane, and abusive.*

In this diverse world, it is crucial to be sensitive to cultures while delivering any form of communication and this further encompasses religions, denominations, and beliefs of others. One must be well versed with the values, norms, and customs of the community they are to deliver their communication; this allows them to have effective communication, and avoid humiliation, and disrespect of people and their cultures, religions, and beliefs. Things such as generalized conclusions and assumptions must be avoided for better information delivery because they portray stereotyping and division of people rather than unity. A better way is to find information that will allow you to foster and strive for inclusivity and understanding. Above all, one must be appreciative and in possession of gratitude while communicating and this involves acknowledging other's contributions, skills, and efforts with sincere compliments which enables a positive rapport and strengthens relationships.

Listening

People often confuse listening and hearing. Hearing involves the use of ears to collect the sounds and words from the environment and making sense of them through brain interpretation. Listening is not just a simple act of hearing sounds, words, or tones but it is an essential etiquette of life that is required to be cultivated through practice and consistency. ***Listening encompasses the ability to understand, respect, and be empathetic of what is being heard and give at most focus.*** *In this fast-paced world where technology and science have peaked, the art of listening has been undervalued due to quick responses, digital distractions, and increased visualization of data and information. Mastering the skill of attentive listening can however significantly enhance one's personal and professional relationships, promote effective communication and foster a harmonious society. A lot of people often ask themselves why they would listen so keenly and critically to a speech or someone speaking when they can record or find the recording after the session and re-listen to it. The simple answer to this question lies in the core of the skill of listening, it involves giving one's full attention to the person speaking not just the ears but also the mind, heart and observing their expressions which can be* *physical or even verbal.*

The ability of someone to set aside perceptions, biases, and distractions and focus solely on the speaker's words, tone, and non-verbal cues makes the art of listening remarkable. Being an active listener makes one to be present in the moment and it creates a safe and supportive space for speakers to express their ideas and ideologies well. A lot of people don't realize that listening establishes a genuine connection with the speaker and listeners by signaling the value of the speaker's thoughts; we also confer respect on their feelings and experiences. A relatively higher percentage of people who engage in active listening are trustworthy and they express high levels of encouragement for others and openness allowing them to honestly communicate with others. This occurs when the listeners understand the speaker's perspective allowing them to develop empathy and deeper insight into the needs, desires, and concerns of the speaker. This becomes a building block for meaningful relationships and resolving conflicts in societies. From a professional perspective such as workplace, educational institutions, and even public platforms, listening plays a crucial role leading to improved collaboration, innovation, and problem-solving. Through attentive listening to colleagues, students, constituents, and others we gain a diverse perspectives of ideas and solutions allowing them to identify common grounds and mutually beneficial solutions to an existing challenge.

Being a good listener also boosts one's leadership skills such as trust, morale, and teamwork. The etiquette of listening extends beyond individual interactions to broader societal contexts because it promotes inclusivity and understanding. By actively seeking out and attentively listening to diverse voices, we can broaden our horizons, challenge our assumptions and promote social justice. For example, listening to marginalized societies allows us to grasp their experiences and concerns allowing the creation of opportunities for positive change and collective progress. One can follow this strategy to obtain better listening skills; by practicing mindfulness and self-awareness through being conscious of one's own listening habits and biases followed by recognizing situations when we are not ready to listen to avoid wasting people's time. When one decides to listen to one's speech or talk, one should try as much as possible to be patient and non-judgemental which allows the speaker to express themselves fully without interruption and premature assumptions. Above all, one must reflect on what has been said and ask thoughtful questions for clarity and understanding; this demonstrates engagement and commitment to one's talk. This strategy is not simple and can not achieve in a day, however, it is essential to understand that one must keep continuous practice of this strategy to obtain better results.

Empathy

Understanding and sharing the feelings of others in a particular situation is what is basically known as empathy, however, our ability to show sympathy and empathy is what makes us humans and it is therefore a fundamental etiquette of life. Empathy allows us to ***connect deeply****,* ***show compassion****, and build* ***harmonious relationships*** *with others in society. This is essential for personal growth, and social interactions. It also leads to the creation of a more inclusive society. Different people express feelings differently. While some may stay calm, non-expressive and silent when faced with a tragedy, others sob, cry, talk, or fight. Among those people who will be silent, some get lost (****state of abandonment****), and broken. The ability of one to show empathy is hugely determined by one's ability to sympathize with the person and understand the magnitude of the situation. This begins with one's willingness to step outside of their experiences and perspectives. Also, when one tries and is truly committed to put themselves in someone else's shoes (situation at the time). One must recognize and validate their emotions even if they differ from the sufferer's own emotions. This allows them to* ***acknowledge*** *and* ***understand*** *the feelings of others. Through this, we can know the appropriate response that will* *be **compassionate** and **supportive**. Here are some of the different ways one can cultivate empathy in life.*

Active listening: *As mentioned in the previous section of "Listening"; attentive listening without judgment is key to understanding one's experience and emotions. A person has to give full attention to the person in a situation while they talk to them or express their feelings, and putting genuine interest is key because it allows them to understand that you are actively participating and absorbing their talk. This allows them to have a safe space to express themselves.*

Perspective-taking: *A person can try to practice the ability to imagine themselves in one's situation by considering different aspects such as background, beliefs, and values. Some people think that because they have a roof over their heads, get three meals every day, and have access to education whatsoever, it's they pass through difficult times when they encounter challenges not knowing that some people have no access to such privileges in their life, but they are grateful for what is there. Therefore, when one imagines a situation where they don't have what they have or they have what they don't have, it allows them to obtain empathy in their hearts and this can help them gain a* *broader understanding of their circumstances and of others allowing them to respond with greater empathy and sensitivity.*

***Self-reflection**: This tool allows us to examine our own emotions, motivations, and biases in life allowing us to develop a deeper understanding of ourselves. With this in practice, one can obtain a highly empathetic lifestyle because they are aware of their own feelings and how they might influence their interactions with others. Some people are ruthless by nature while others are sympathetic by nature, if the two people practice self-reflection, the degree of empathy developed might vary but they will both have a clear understanding of their feelings allowing them to know their stand in a given situation.*

***Kindness and compassion:** Our daily interactions with others through various situations and events allow us to cultivate empathy. This is through various acts such as kindness (offering a helping hand or a word of encouragement) can create a significant impact on one's life and well-being. Most of these acts are empathetic which is innate and allows us to create a positive ripple effect hence inspiring others to do the same. They say charity begins at home and thus if a home is filled with empathetic actions, children in that home will* *have empathy in their life and the opposite is true.*

Lastly one can seek out diverse experiences and perspectives which can allow them to enhance their empathetic character. These can come from engaging with people of diverse backgrounds, cultures, and walks of life which exposes us to a wider range of experiences, and this challenges our biases and assumptions. For all these, one gets an extended understanding of human experiences and promotes a more inclusive worldview. It is, however, necessary for one to understand that practicing an empathetic lifestyle requires patience and willingness to learn and grow.

Respect

*I am sure everyone has heard of the notion that "**Respect is only earned but not forced**" Hence I stand firm to say that respect is a fundamental etiquette of life. It involves recognizing the **inherent worth**, **dignity**, and **rights** of all individuals. Respect is a complex action that builds a foundation for healthy relationships, effective communication, and a harmonious society. When one gives respect to both themselves and others, it not only benefits them and others in society but also enhances their own personal growth and well-being. Respecting one's self and others doesn't come out of the blue but rather it begins with acknowledging and appreciating the uniqueness and values of every person. This takes in account the differences in beliefs, religion, culture, ethnicity, opinions, and backgrounds. This alone allows one to treat others with courtesy, kindness, and consideration. Through listening to other people's perspectives , opinions and arguments whether you disagree or not, also engaging in constructive dialogue instead of hostility or dismissiveness. It is, however, essential to practice empathy (we talked about it in the previous section above) as you work on building a respectiful life. This allows us to understand and share the feelings of others making us to obtain a sense of connection and compassion.*

Furthermore, one needs to be a good communicator, and listener. As these provide You (them) with the skills needed for putting themselves in one's shoes and seeking to understand their situation or experiences.

The above skillset allows us to develop a greater appreciation of other people's perspectives, experiences, and situations which helps us to demonstrate respect in our relationships and interactions with them. In this evolving world, having a purely respective personality entails someone having value for diversity and promoting inclusivity. This allows the recognition and embrace of the richness of different cultures, backgrounds, and races which helps us to create a more tolerant and accepting society. Being that all humans belong to one race "The Human race" we also have other sub-categories such as Asians, Africans, Europeans etcetera. Respecting everyone's rage, cultures, and backgrounds through acknowledging their existence, values, and norms (Diversity) helps in building a robust and tolerant society where everyone is welcomed and loved. The process of seeking out opportunities to learn about and engage with diverse perspectives leads to the expansion of our understanding and it also challenges any prejudices or biases we may hold setting us free and tolerant. However much we want to have a diverse community of people, we must also understand that treating other people's boundaries and autonomy with care is very important.

This means recognizing and honoring one's physical, emotional, and psychological limits through simple acts such as seeking permission, and consent, and refraining from disrespectful and invasive behavior. Furthermore, we need to acknowledge people's rights to make their own choices and decisions regardless of their results. Sometimes these decisions might differ from ours but we must respect them and share our point of view allowing us to liaise with each other to make a clearly informed decision. I want to inform you my readers that, respect extends beyond individual interactions to encompass broader societal values and norms. We can look at the environment, being mindful of the ecological impact and making sustainable choices with respect, the laws and regulations in most of our communities demonstrate our commitment to a just and orderly society. By recognizing and adhering to these regulations and norms we all contribute to the well-being of and harmony of our communities. Like other social interaction etiquettes, to cultivate respect one requires self-reflection and commitment to personal growth. This takes into account the evaluation and recognition of our own biases, prejudices, and assumptions and taking a step further to challenge them so that we foster an inclusive mindset. When we develop good self-awareness skills, we recognize when we may be acting in a disrespectful manner and also empowers us to make conscious choices to change the behavior.

FIVE

PROFESSIONAL SUCCESS.

*We often use the term "Professional success" to describe the achievements and fulfilment of one's experiences in their professional life or career. This encompasses a wide range of accomplishments which vary greatly depending on the individual's goals, aspirations, and measures of success. Various factors and concepts are considered when it comes to professional success such as goal setting, continuous learning, hard work and persistence, relationships, adaptability and flexibility, emotional intelligence, work-life balance, and risk-taking to mention but a few. In this chapter, we will talk about the four major etiquettes that lead to professional success in life which can be memorized by the acronym "**TANA**" meaning **T**ime-Management, **A**ccountability, **N**etworking, and **A**daptability. Before we dive*

deeper into TANA let's first understand what really professional success is and what are the different aspects that make a professionally successful person. At first one needs to understand the profession they are passionate about and this can be done by setting a smart goal, learning about the professions, building relationships, and others. We discussed what a smart goal is and how to set one so I request you to first understand that section.

The relevance of goal setting is to establish a clear and achievable target through specific objectives which allow one to focus their efforts and develop a proper road map for progress. Along the way, one keeps learning new skills which can be lifelong skills that allow one to stay up to date with the industry trends, and seek opportunities for professional development. Even though all this is feasible, hard work and persistence are highly required and this makes one dedicated, with a strong work ethic allowing them to overcome challenges and stay motivated to achieve their set goals. As we will discuss in the later sub-sections, networking, and building relationships are vital which most people forget during their professional development career and thus end up unsuccessful. One has to develop strong professional relationships and networks which can significantly contribute to their decision-making, execution, and developmental success.

This can be through building rapport with colleagues, mentors, and industry professionals whose guidance, support, and opportunities are valuable for your professional development. A lot of people have fallen from the peak of their professional success due to poor emotional management hence one needs to be acquainted with emotional intelligence skills which allows them to manage their emotions effectively.

This can help them navigate relationships, communicate effectively and make sound informed decisions in their professional career. At times people sacrifice their well-being for professional success and many times they end up using their accumulated wealth from their profession to restore their well-being which sometimes doesn't get restored. To avoid this, one must have a work-life balance and this allows them to maintain their physical and mental wellbeing for sustained success. Staying up late for the research proposal for one's next big fund securement might seem an ideal thing to do but also continuous lack of sleep will lead to health deterioration and one might start getting insomnia, hallucinations, and other psychiatric diseases. Finally, we have to understand that having a professional career or success is not something that one trek alone hence a lot of collaboration and leadership is required, and these skills allow us to work well with others. Skills such as effective communication (we discussed this in our previous chapter under subsection communication, you might want to revisit it for more clarity), teamwork and the ability to inspire and motivate others have a significant impact on increasing one's career opportunities.

As all leaders and entrepreneurs are risk-takers, the ability to be a risk-taker catalyzes one's professional success because it allows us to step out of our comfort zone, forcing us to embrace new challenges and seize opportunities however, the uncertainty; this could further lead to breakthroughs and accelerated success. Understanding that success is subjective and varies from person to person, it is very important for one to define what success means to them and then establish clear metrics for measuring the progress. Things such as career milestones, job satisfaction, financial achievements, and making an impact (positive) in the field or society can be measures of professional success. Since you have gotten a clear picture of success, let's look at ***TANA****s, which I have briefly described as the most priority factors for professional success (etiquettes or principles). The four principles above when adhered to can help one to navigate their careers with integrity, professionalism, and effectiveness.*

Time Management

Time is a resource for everyone, we don't pay for it, but we use it. I believe everything we use must be accounted for in our life. I am certain that everyone has a limited amount of time on earth, we just don't know how much. I am always fascinated by one of the famous sayings about time by William Penn he once said and I quote, ***"Time is what we need most but it's what we use worst."*** *I know, everyone has their own understanding of this quote, and also hear me out, with regards to time, we always crave and yarn for more time or we regret perhaps we had more time maybe we would have done something to prevent the bad results of the present however the time was there and we never saw it a relevant resource till it got exhausted. The value of each second or minute can only be understood when it's gone because every fraction of time that goes into one's life, will never come back. I know many of you will criticize my analogy about the quote above, but I find it fascinating because we always claim not to have time yet the time is always there but we use it inappropriately. Time management is an essential tool for professional success because it allows us to prioritize tasks, set deadlines, and develop strong organizational skills which allow us to meet our commitments and maximize productivity.*

The benefits of time management encompass improved productivity because one gets to make the most of their work hours through prioritizing tasks and setting clear goals and this allows them to allocate appropriate time for each activity. Many professionals focus on high-value tasks allowing them to eliminate time-wasting activities and this maintains their steady pace of work and leads to increased output and accomplishments. The process further helps them to meet deadlines such as projects, meetings, and research which are crucial to their profession. Through this procrastination is prevented and deliverables are completed on schedule which increases their reputation, reliability, and overall success. We often witness people have work stress and anxiety and most of the time it's due to poor time management thus one has to master the skill of effective time management for a healthier work-life balance. Proper time management reduces last-minute rushes, and excessive workloads and maintains a sustainable pace which helps in reducing stress and anxiety at work allowing one to make better decisions and increased focus which promotes one's overall health and wellbeing which are essential for long-term professional success.

Another thing about this is that it gives one a way forward on how to identify the most effective way to complete tasks, one will have enough time to streamline the tasks, eliminate unnecessary steps and then utilize the most effective time-saving techniques to accomplish the tasks. For this, many professionals have been observed to accomplish more in less time and this boosts their productivity allowing them to take on more additional responsibilities and seize new professions for better professional growth and success. We all need a milestone for reputation and ethical work, one way people have achieved this success milestone is through effective time management allowing them to be consistent, deliver high-quality work, and have quality time for themselves. This skill makes people reliable, organized, and dependable and with such a reputation, doors of career advancements open, also increased responsibilities and trust from colleagues and superiors, this paves the way for making the person obtain milestones that can be used as a measure of their success. With a huge level of prioritization in one's professional life, distractions and interruptions are minimized which allows them to maintain high levels of focus and concentration allowing them to produce quality work with greater accuracy, creativity, and problem-solving abilities.

Sometimes one also needs to look at what their efforts have yielded, and the way to do this is through self-reflection which can only be possible if someone has good skills in time management. With self-reflection, one gets enough information about their set-goal status and also gets time to identify new opportunities as this act creates space for strategic thinking and planning. Many professionals have been able to identify areas for improvement, and growth which have allowed them to pursue professional development initiatives and seize emerging opportunities that align with their career aspirations. We often witness a lot of procrastination in college students and some other requests for more time or extension of deadlines for assignment submission. This is all due to poor time management but not increased workload. As students, we often have the notion that we still have plenty of time. Take an example a literature assignment in which the lecturer gives to read the book "win your inner battles" It is about one hundred and thirty pages and slow readers can take around twenty hours making ten days with two hours reading every day. The lecturer will give the assignment time as three weeks which is sufficient for everyone. However, some people will want to read the book and do the assignment in the last three days.

While others will make themselves busy with other activities such as physical exercise, partying etcetera. These activities are not time wasters because having assignments doesn't mean depriving of one's free and enjoyable time. The problem is time management, instead of spending five hours at a late-night party someone could budget three hours for the party and two hours for the assignment; instead of playing basketball the whole weekend, one can budget one and a half hours every weekend for the assignment and other forms. This way one can work on many tasks with no lag in each making effective use of time and reducing the propaganda of not having the time or less time given for the task.

Accountability

Most of the time we hear people telling us to be responsible and make informed decisions so that we are accountable for the results of the actions and decisions we make. Accountability simply means to be responsible for actions, decisions, and their outcomes which include successes and failures that come through our decisions and actions (verbal or nonverbal). It also encompasses two other strong notions of learning from our own mistakes and striving to have continuous improvement in our life. This demonstrates reliability and maturity in society. This etiquette is fundamental for professional growth and social interaction in communities because it allows the promotion of personal responsibility, reliability, and integrity in the workspace, community, and peers. One must understand the beauty of having this ethical and social virtue. First and foremost, this etiquette helps one build trust and credibility as it allows one to establish a good and reliable personality among peers, colleagues, superiors, and clients. Taking ownership of one's actions through commitments and accepting their faults and learning from them makes them earn respect and confidence in others.

This later is a key to building a successful relationship and fostering collaboration in different aspects of life such as work, society, and religion. With this comes another goodness through which enhanced performance and results are yielded. This is because the person possessing this virtue is driven to best performances in all settings whether work or societal matters. This goes further in the professional side when the professionals take ownership of their tasks and projects allowing them to be accountable for all the risks and successes of their work, they are more likely to invest in necessary efforts and attention to deliver high-quality work. We must know that accountability as the etiquette of life drives commitment to excellence and improved performances leading to achieving the desired goals and results while having no ego. Accountability as an etiquette of life is the only virtue that emphasizes more about self-reflection and learning from one's mistakes. This leads to improved problem-solving skills. Through acknowledging and learning from our mistakes, we ***leave*** *the system of shifting the blame on others. By this we learn to accept the results of our actions (errors or successes). In the long run, we allow ourselves to focus on finding the solutions.*

By being self-aware of our actions, we also develop mitigation programsn that allows us in preventing the already experienced challenges in the near future. This allows us to be firm and strong than trying to hide in the safe zone. With this mindset, we improve our personal growth and professionalism leading to success in life. In a broader view, one equipped with the etiquette of accountability shows a high degree of consistency in which they always try harder to learn from the failures and mistakes they make which allows them to obtain new strategies and mitigations to doing things better which makes them reliable and dependable. This allows them to build a strong positive reputation and opens more doors to new opportunities. Most people are observed and evidenced to be effective communicators because they are open and transparent through their honest nature and this forces them to share progress updates and seek assistance or clarification when needed. The character also calls to seek feedback, identify areas of improvement, and invest in new skills and knowledge leading to self-improvement and competency. Individuals who embody accountability in their leadership set a positive example for others. When leaders take responsibility for their actions, admit mistakes, and work towards solutions, they inspire and motivate their teams. Accountability becomes contagious, fostering a culture of responsibility and trust that drives collective success.

Networking

*Networking is a crucial factor in achieving professional success. In my country and some others I willway, they have a very old notion which says "**Do you know somebody ,who knows somebody in a given place you are pursuing for success?**" In some cases we call this corrusption or favouritism but its **Networking** . In this process, we are tpically trying to build relationships, knowledge exchange, career opportunities, personal growth ,and building a support system. During this process we are aiming at creating and nurturing relationships, its not just about what others an do foe you but also what they can get from you. The networks we make in our life, depending on how genuine they are, they can land us to menorshiop, collaboration and new suitable opportunities. Its a well known notion that there is no absolutness in knowledge hence, veryone has something they know more than the other. As we connect with people, we gain alot of insights, advice and information from each other regardless our fields of life. It can be helpful as it keeps uptodate on industry trends, best practices and new technologies. In many good reputabel companies where many of us desire to work, they less advertise their job openings publically because even the existing workers are looking forward to grabbing these chances.*

In my culture we say that if you are giving gifts; the moment you start with the neigbour's house, *there is a high chance that many of your family members will never get some of these gifts. My grandmother used to tell me when ever I served something and started with other people, "**You have put food in the nose and forgot the mouth?**" Which was a parable to mean that when ever opportunities come your way, start with yourself before you give the neigbours. Networking gives us access to hidden job markets, where through a word of mouth you can learn about the available positions in a given company or personal referrals. Okay, alot might ask bout personal growth through networking. When we interact with many different people "**Diversity**" with different professional background, we cultivate the power of communication, confidence and perspective understanding (empathy and sympathy). Also the networks one makes, can be a strong support system for them providing guidance, encouragement and assistance when needed. Some people in the networks we create can turn out to be our advisors who can invest into our success. Furhtermore, Your professional reputation gets enhanced with a good network because as you become well connected, and respected it allows you to showcase your skills, expertise and character to a broader audience.*

How to embarck on Networking Journey

If am to be realistic, some of the difficult steps in professional development isNetworking. Its always hard to understand where to start and how to start. Most times people study and end up at the peak of their education without a good network thus its hard for them to land on their first beating job. Lucky you the readers of this book, we can try to ook through the strategies used to create a good professional network.

Build and nurture professional networks: As a seeker of professional development, it is very useful to attend industry events, conferences, join relevant associations, and establish connections with peers, mentors, and influencers. This with give you a very good exposure to the people in different fields, with different perspective, like manded ones and those who can find value in you as well. This is also known as self-presentation advertisement, in this type of networking you are the product of your own self, and it will allow you to survey for your market potential and will provide you with the opportunities for career advancement, learning, and exposure to new opportunities.

Collaboration: As a person looking for a good networking strategy emphasize working with a team, a well established mentor and collaboration to achieve collective goals. The more you are in team working, it allows you to undertake a journey of self-discovery, locate the like minds, learn how to manage stress, deadlines and cultivates your reliability powert. From thes activities, you can spot who you can network with and same happens to those in your team, or collab. When you ensure to be good team member, you foster positive relationships with colleagues, contribute to a supportive work environment, and become open to different ideas and perspectives. Above all, you are going to harness the power of productivity, innovation, and these will pave your path to professional growth and success.

Importance of Networking.

Networking etiquette plays a vital role in professional success by facilitating connections, building relationships, and creating opportunities for growth and advancement. Embracing effective networking etiquette can greatly influence professional success in the following ways:

Expanded Opportunities: *Networking etiquette allows individuals to expand their professional connections beyond their immediate circles. By actively engaging with colleagues, industry professionals, and potential mentors, individuals increase their visibility and access* *to a broader range of opportunities. These opportunities may include job openings, collaborative projects, promotions, and valuable insights into industry trends and developments.*

Relationship Building: *Networking etiquette emphasizes building genuine relationships based on mutual respect, trust, and reciprocity. By actively listening, showing interest, and offering support to others, individuals can establish meaningful connections. Strong relationships built through networking can lead to referrals, recommendations, and valuable partnerships, which in turn can enhance professional success.*

Knowledge and Information Sharing: *Networking provides opportunities to exchange knowledge, insights, and information. Engaging in professional conversations, attending industry events, and participating in networking groups or online communities enables individuals to stay updated on the latest trends, innovations, and best practices in their field. Access to valuable information and diverse perspectives can enhance professional competence and contribute to success.*

Career Guidance and Mentorship: *Effective networking etiquette allows individuals to seek* *guidance and mentorship from more experienced professionals. Engaging with mentors can provide invaluable advice, support, and guidance in navigating career challenges, setting goals, and making informed decisions. Mentors can offer insights and share their experiences, enabling individuals to make better-informed choices and accelerate their professional growth.*

Collaborative Opportunities: *Networking etiquette fosters a collaborative mindset, encouraging individuals to seek opportunities for cooperation and partnership. By connecting with professionals from complementary fields or with diverse expertise, individuals can leverage collective strengths, share resources, and collaborate on projects or initiatives. Collaborative efforts enhance professional success by allowing individuals to tackle complex challenges, access new markets, and achieve mutually beneficial outcomes.*

Professional Development: *Networking etiquette often involves attending industry conferences, seminars, and workshops. These events offer opportunities for professional development through learning from experts, participating in panel discussions, and engaging in workshops. Networking with peers and industry leaders can provide access to* *specialized knowledge and skills, promoting personal growth and enhancing professional success.*

Industry Visibility and Personal Branding: *Active networking helps individuals enhance their professional visibility and build a strong personal brand. By attending events, contributing to industry discussions, and sharing insights on professional platforms, individuals can establish themselves as thought leaders and experts in their field. A positive personal brand increases credibility and opens doors for career advancement and new opportunities.*

Support and Collaboration during Career Transitions: *Networking etiquette establishes a support system that can be invaluable during career transitions. Whether seeking new employment, exploring entrepreneurship, or pursuing career changes, a strong professional network can provide advice, recommendations, and connections that facilitate a smooth transition. Support from the network helps individuals navigate challenges and increases the likelihood of successful transitions.*

Adaptability

Adaptability, it is always coupled with flexibility which in many life journies has been noted to be the ***key*** *to the* ***path to long-term success****. We can define adaptability as the ability to* ***adapt*** *to* ***changing circumstances*** *and* ***embrace new challenges*** *in the journey of life. It is crucial and a key factor in one's life whose aim is to foster long-term success. Being* ***open to new ideas****,* ***approaches****, and* ***technologies*** *allows you to harness the ulitmate power to professionalism and to maintain and remain relevant making you able to seize emerging opportunities. Adaptability etiquette, is far beyond changing ability but it can be understood as the ability to* ***adjust*** *and* ***thrive*** *in changing circumstances. If you look at the peripheral point of view, it the two might look similar but one is progressive while the other is stablizing. Adaptability etiquette is essential for professional success in today's* ***dynamic*** *and* ***evolving*** *work environments. By embracing adaptability etiquette, individuals can greatly influence their professional success in some of the following ways:*

Embracing Change: *Adaptability etiquette involves* ***being open*** *and* ***receptive*** *to change. Instead of resisting or fearing change,* *adaptable professionals embrace it as an opportunity for growth and improvement. This mindset allows individuals to navigate transitions, industry shifts, and emerging trends, positioning them for success in an ever-changing professional landscape. I remember many times in my country when new tools were introduced in schools or factories, many employees who never took the advantage of learning the new tools were fired but those who were alert and decided to learn the new tools kept their jobs. Also in today's world, when a company adopts new software, an adaptable employee takes the initiative to learn and master the new system, becoming a valuable resource for their team. Think about how you in any sector you are and at any stage of your professional success, how can you view upcoming changes in your workplace as opportunities for personal and professional growth? It will always help you to keep accepting change and adjust as you thrive together with long-term growth.*

Flexibility and Resilience: *Adaptable professionals demonstrate flexibility and resilience in the face of challenges and setbacks. When you develop the ability and willingness to adjust approaches, strategies, and goals as needed, this ability enables You to overcome obstacles, recover from failures, and bounce back stronger. Resilience is a valuable trait for* *professional success, as it allows individuals to persevere, maintain productivity, and find creative solutions. The sad thing is that developing this value is hard as walking on hot-coal-raod. It so happens to many of us that after any failure be it a project, research or any kind, we tend to think of it as the end of the road and never understand that every ending gives birth to a new beginning. Resilient professionals will always quickly regroup, analyze where they went wrong and devise a new strategy to stand up again and aim for the next targets of sucess. Ask your self every time you feel down professionally, how can you develope new strategies to harness the resilience for better handling setbacks in your career? This might seem to look like a simple question but the more its being asked in your inner self, the more opinions you will get and one of those will be the answer you are looking for.*

Learning Agility: *Adaptability etiquette fosters a commitment to* ***continuous learning*** *and improvement. One time I was walking in one of my university where I studied, and I was suprised when I saw "**Center for continious education**." I was suprised and it kept ringing in my ears and when I asked one of my friends in the working section, he told me that when you think education ends once you get a good job or sit in a good office and earn a good pay-check, you are wrong. He further taught me how* *growth is calculated, it can be vertricle or horizontal and depending what one is looking for in their career, they take different paths. But what stroke me was the last words he said. He said that, "**Adaptive professioal growth is initiated intrinsically by the ability of one to desire continious education**." Adaptable professionals are eager to acquire new skills, knowledge, and perspectives. They seek opportunities for professional development, stay updated on industry trends, and embrace lifelong learning. Learning agility enhances professional competence, keeps individuals relevant, and positions them for new opportunities. Taking online courses in your free time is one way of embracing adaptive professional continious learning and it is always useful because it keeps one updated with the latest industrial, clinical, name it developments.*

*There is a notion in my country; the qualifications you have together with your network, can land you on your dream job or burry you. Its only skilsl and increased knowledge enhancement that will keep you on that dream job. When I published on my LinkedIn picture statement and I wrote "**Let your skills speak**", I was asked by many of my friends that why I chose that title. Anyways the asnwer is simple, the only way to show that you are good at what you do than what your papers* *"speak" is by showing it in practicle however, the only way to be better than anyone who can do what you do is to be multi-skilled and diverse in knowledge.*

Problem-Solving and Innovation: *Adaptable professionals excel in problem-solving and innovation. Ones ability to encounter a problem and lay down possible solutions to it is a skill known as* ***problem solving*** *however, the ability to analyze a problem and come up with new soulutions from scratch is known as* ***innovative solving****. Adaptive professionals possess the ability to think critically, analyze situations, and generate creative solutions. By adapting their thinking and approaches to new challenges, they find innovative ways to address complex problems and meet evolving demands. This adaptability fosters a reputation for resourcefulness and positions individuals as valuable assets in their organizations. There are many examples on this topic of adaptive problem solving. Imagine you as the CEO of a company and the resources have come to shortage, what could be the best solution? Someone might devise a cost-effective solution that maintains project quality and deadlines while another person will find an alternative sustainable source of resources for increased productivity and adaptibility. However, all solutions might seem to be better but the matter of time affects them.*

Before you think about the solutions to anything first ask yourself, How could you cultivate an innovative mindset to solve complex challenges in your work place? In summary, adaptability etiquette is a crucial factor in professional success. By embracing change, demonstrating flexibility, cultivating learning agility, problem-solving creatively, adopting new technologies, excelling in interpersonal skills, making agile decisions, and maintaining a growth mindset, individuals can thrive in dynamic work environments and position themselves for long-term success.

SIX

RELATIONSHIPS

Etiquette plays a pivotal role in the tapestry of human relationships. These principles act as the threads that weave together interactions, fostering respect, understanding, and harmony. In the complex web of human connections, etiquette serves as the foundational framework that guides our behaviors and interactions, ensuring that relationships are built and maintained on a bedrock of mutual respect and consideration. Relationships often come unexpectedly, but they are sustained and nurtured through a set of principles known as relationship etiquette. It's not surprising that we occasionally witness relationships falter simply because one or two of these binding principles are neglected. This neglect can lead to misunderstandings, conflicts, and ultimately, the deterioration of what could have been enduring connections. The essence of how humans form and sustain relationships is deeply ingrained in these principles. Friendship, love, family, societies, and communities are all made up of relationships. These relationships are the building blocks of our social fabric, and the way we navigate them is largely influenced by our adherence to etiquette. Etiquette helps us to express our respect and appreciation for others, creating an environment where positive and meaningful interactions can flourish.

Whether it's saying "please" and "thank you," listening attentively, or showing empathy, these small acts of etiquette contribute significantly to the health and longevity of our relationships. It's not that we fall for those who are closely connected to us by chance, but rather, we are naturally drawn to those who demonstrate respect for our moral and behavioral principles. We tend to form lasting bonds with individuals who acknowledge and uphold the values that are important to us. This mutual respect is the cornerstone of any healthy relationship, as it fosters a sense of trust and security. Consider a scenario in the workplace: a team member who consistently shows respect for their colleagues' ideas and efforts is likely to be valued and trusted. Their adherence to workplace etiquette—such as being punctual, meeting deadlines, and communicating effectively—creates a positive and collaborative work environment. This, in turn, enhances team cohesion and productivity. In social settings, etiquette plays a crucial role in facilitating smooth and enjoyable interactions. For example, being mindful of table manners during a dinner party not only shows respect for the host but also ensures that everyone has a pleasant dining experience.

Similarly, in family relationships, simple acts of courtesy—such as showing appreciation for each other's efforts and communicating openly—strengthen the bonds of love and support. Moreover, in romantic relationships, etiquette helps to build and maintain a strong emotional connection. Acts of kindness, thoughtful gestures, and effective communication are all elements of relationship etiquette that contribute to a loving and supportive partnership. These actions show that we value and respect our partner, which is essential for the relationship to thrive. In communities and societies, etiquette serves as a guiding principle for harmonious living. It helps us navigate diverse cultural norms and practices, promoting inclusivity and respect for differences. By adhering to community etiquette, we contribute to creating a cohesive and supportive environment where everyone feels valued and respected.

Respect and Courtesy.

Respect and courtesy form the bedrock of any meaningful relationship. This means we can not form a solid or useful relationship without the foundation of respect. These two principles encapsulate a wide array of behaviors that signal appreciation for another person's presence, thoughts, and emotions. In relationships, respect manifests as a recognition of the inherent worth of the other person. It doesnt matter which type of relationship one is in, but the main thing is when you respect one's worth, you are aiding in propergation and maintainance of the realtion. It is one way of showing how important and useful the person or people you are in a relationship with in your life. It is an acknowledgment that their views, feelings, and experiences are valid, even if they differ from your own. Its so hard to understand diversity in people and opinion therefore cultivating the abiltiy to duley respect and accept people's differences. Respect and courtesy are not just about grand gestures but are often found in the small, everyday interactions. This includes listening attentively when someone speaks, acknowledging their contributions, and valuing their time and effort.

Courtesy, on the other hand, refers to the behaviors that express this respect. It involves using polite language, showing gratitude, and being considerate of others' needs and feelings. These principles help prevent conflicts and misunderstandings by promoting a culture of mutual appreciation and care. When people feel respected, they are more likely to open up and communicate honestly, fostering deeper connections and trust. Trying to practice the following activities, one can ensure that they cultivate good sense of respect and courtesy for others:

Active Listening: *This means fully concentrating, understanding, and responding thoughtfully to what is being said. A lot of times, when we engage in conversations, or interactions with people we care about, its we tend to be relactant at listening to them; this makes them not understood and we end up not fully engaging with them. Avoid interrupting or thinking about your response while the other person is speaking. The challenge is that when you try to interrupt or think about what your response is, chances are you are going to screw everything. Instead, show that you are engaged by nodding, maintaining eye contact, and occasionally summarizing what they have said. One might think that its pretence, but higher chances that one is going to understand and get fully emersed in one's converstational moments.*

Polite Language: *Incorporate words like "please," "thank you," and "excuse me" into your daily interactions. I think we have already talked about this in details but lets say it again. Polite language helps create a safe and friendly environment for people around you. It is a very core aspect in relationships and makes many worst situations that would have destroyed the relationship mend and firm it. These simple words can soften requests, show appreciation, and smooth over potential misunderstandings. They signal to others that you are considerate and respectful. Of course, as the notion goes,* *when you respect it doesnt mean you have to be respected back but the results of your respectful actions are more sounding than the respect you might expect to get in return.*

Non-verbal Cues: *Communication is not just about words; your body language plays a crucial role as well. If you read the chapters before, you will understand that most times we communicate more with our non-verbals than by verbal coms. People in our cicles are more vigilant and reading of our non-verbal communications than what we say. One can be sweet by word of mouth but when they are your worst enemy and its hard to notice unless you are going to consider reading their non-verbal coms. This such as maintaining eye contact shows that you are interested and present in the conversation. Smiling can make others feel at ease and welcomed. Avoid crossing your arms, as this can be perceived as defensive or disinterested. Instead, adopt an open posture that invites communication. Additionally, showing respect and courtesy involves being punctual, as it demonstrates that you value others' time. Apologizing sincerely when you are wrong and showing empathy for others' experiences also reinforce these principles. By consistently practicing these behaviors, you create a positive and respectful environment that nurtures healthy relationships.*

Honesty and Transparency.

Honesty and transparency are the pillars of trust in any relationship. In our previous chapters we have discussed about turst and somewhere we talked about honesty as well. Lets dive more into it as a core and a fundermental pillar of any form of relationship. These two principles ensure that interactions are based on truthfulness and openness, which are essential for building and maintaining trust. Trust is the cornerstone of any relationship, whether personal or professional. It allows individuals to feel secure in their interactions and confident that their partner or colleague has their best interests at heart. Honesty involves being truthful about your thoughts, feelings, and actions. You will find many people coining the word honesty with other words to create a clear cut between truths. Some might use words such as honest truth, honest speech and others. All these request for different forms of audience and truths. The audience of one's relationship matters and this creates the degree of honesty that they have. This however fundermentally mean that one has not to be hiding or distorting the truth, even when it is uncomfortable. Transparency takes honesty a step further which is hard to cultivate and most people can be honest but not transparent.

Transparency ensures that there is openness and clarity in communication. It involves sharing relevant information and being clear about intentions and expectations. These principles help prevent misunderstandings and conflicts, as everyone involved is operating with the same set of facts and expectations. However, its very hard to find such an ideal relationship setting whether in homes, industries or any form of societal setting but if at least they are being emphasized and individuals try hard to embed them in their everyday life, they can foster a sense of safety and security, as individuals know they can rely on each other to be truthful and open. One can try to cultivate honesty and transparency by making use of these forms of soft skills:

Open Communication: *Instill an environment in either your community, society, relationship or work place where people are always encouraged and free to communicate freely. This will help them to foster an atmosphere where open communication is felt and valued. This means being willing to share your thoughts and feelings, even when they are difficult or uncomfortable. I know this is an environment which is not easy to create because we have lots of differences both intra and inter-personal, however one person once said that the highest level of strength one can ever cultivate is to* *allow himself to agree on the disagreement. It actuall doesnt make sense in the first catch but when you give it time it does. Agreeing on a disagreement means that one respects other people's opinions and acknowledges the existance of diversity. By this one encourages others to do the same and give a listening audience without judgment.*

Admitting Mistakes: *Recognize that everyone makes mistakes and that admitting them is a sign of strength, not weakness. I remember one day when I was caught by my mother with a nude magazine page. I knew my mother was to flogg me till I was unable to walk and I could bare to accept her to flogg me even if 100 times. But the worst situation came when she took me to my father and I knew my father was gonna wound me more than my mother. The only thing was to lie and destroy all the evidence by eating the magazine page and swallowing all its contents making my mother look like a fool and denying everything. It was the worst time in my childhood, my mother was so furious and beat me with alot of anger that i bled from my nose. However, my father was not furious but he said only few words after that incident and they are the ones I wanna share. After the whole event and I was sleeping in my bed wounded all over my body and nose lifted because I was severly bleeding. He said, "The only mistake you made was to desroy the truth* *and making your mother look a fool infront of someone who believes in her. Admitting mistakes is more beatiful and peaceful than winning because mistakes are forms of growth and we all do them however, winning from mistakes makes you nurture wrongly and the world will do worse than what your mother did. " When you make a mistake, own up to it promptly and take responsibility. This shows integrity and builds trust, as it demonstrates that you are honest and willing to be accountable.*

Setting Clear Boundaries: *Clear and honest communication about boundaries is essential for healthy relationships. It is kinda of a limiting radius for which you and your partner can not cross unless discussed. Actually in societies this is very common and very often what makes a society more strong is setting clear bounderies for every aspect of life. Sometimes it can be observed that bounderies can limit the ability to explore beyond however, being boundaryless is also hard to maintain a healthy and respectful relationship. You can discuss and agree on boundaries early on, and respect them. If boundaries change, communicate this openly and work together to find a mutually acceptable solution. Additionally, honesty and transparency involve being consistent in your words and actions. If you say you will do something, follow through.*

Be honest about your capabilities and limitations, and do not make promises you cannot keep. By practicing these behaviors, you build a foundation of trust and reliability that strengthens your relationships.

Empathy and Compassion.

Empathy and compassion are the glue that holds relationships together, especially during challenging times. We talked alot about empathy and being sympathetic so its better to consider having a revisit of some previous sections and have more understanding of it. Okay, lets see what empathy has to play here. Empathy involves understanding and sharing the feelings of another person. It is the ability to put yourself in someone else's shoes and see the world from their perspective. This is a challenging thing to do because most times when we are looking at how people behave, act or respond to stimuli, we tend to judge quickly. Being empathetic allows one to see the life using s third eye making then have an enhanced ability to have informed decisons and maintain relationships. Compassion, on the other hand, involves not only understanding someone else's feelings but also wanting to alleviate their suffering and provide support. These two qualities are essential for deepening emotional connections and providing meaningful support. We have in life peopel who are known to escalate pain in any form it is in one's life. I remember we used to study with a boy who every time saw that we were going to be punished as a class majorly for making noise or failing exams, he would try to make the whole situation look drammatic and more scarery.

He and his friends used to cut sticks from a guava tree for those of you who dont know the special feature of this tree sticks is that if its well cut in a desired dimensions and thin-long, it can be so painful when used to punish someone. So these boys used to cut them and bring a banch to the class so when the teacher came to punish, they would offer him or her a stick. Such people are pain inflicters and escalaters. Empathy and compassion enable individuals to respond to each other's needs with kindness and understanding, fostering a sense of belonging and security. They help to build strong, resilient relationships that can weather difficult times. Trying few simple actions in life such as the ones below can help you foster a good level of empathy and compassion:

***Putting Yourself in one's Shoes:** Make a conscious effort to see situations from the other person's perspective. One way to do this is to own the challenge being faced by your partner, friend or collegue in a theoretical way then ask yourself how you would feel if you were in their position and what you would need or want. This can help you respond more thoughtfully and empathetically. The response we give to others when they are in difficult situations is sometimes the reason they stay or go away and* *this makes us either the people they can trust, work with or even relay on and the opposite is true.*

Showing Genuine Concern: *Demonstrate that you care about the other person's feelings and well-being. Care is demonstrated in different forms such as physical, emotional and a combination of both. So by making actions that express genuine care and concern in one's life it allows them to understand their worth and your positon in their life. Try by asking how they are feeling, listen to their concerns, and offer support when you are in positon to. Support can be physical, material or emotional. Even small gestures of kindness, such as a comforting word or a thoughtful note, can make a big difference.*

Being Patient: *Recognize that everyone processes emotions and experiences differently. This reminds me of Alan, a boy I studied with in junior school, who was said to process grief emotions late than medically expected. It was suprising to everyone that he has this condition and no one could understand him at school. We bacame friends and it was always strange when ever something bad happened and everyone was in grief he could not show it or even express any sign of grief. We once lost a friend at school who was reported to have bleed after falling in shower and died on the way to the hospital. We* *all were in grief, denied studying for a week, we all had very bad mood and Alan was okay. However we all thought maybe he never knew the girl personally so to him maybe it was just a normal thing but to my suprize the girl was a village mate they knew each other well. Anyways, when Alan's mother died of breast cancer, it was believed that Alan loved his mother so much because all his siblings and his father thought he was an outcust child. Alan was never seen crying or even expressing grief and this was so hard to accept. However, when we got to school after a few days, we looked for Alan and he was no where to be seen. To our dismey, he had locked himself in one toilet crying claiming that his mother was gone and he was left alone in this world.*

It actually took him a week to express the grief emotion of his mother's death. Be patient and give others the time and space they need to work through their feelings. Avoid rushing them or dismissing their emotions. Additionally, empathy and compassion involve being attentive to non-verbal cues and being present in the moment. Practice active listening, not just to respond but to understand. Show that you are engaged and that you value the other person's feelings and experiences. By consistently demonstrating empathy and compassion, you create a supportive and nurturing environment that strengthens your relationships. By expanding on these principles of respect and courtesy, honesty and transparency, and empathy and compassion, you can develop deeper, more meaningful relationships. These principles not only enhance your interactions but also foster a sense of trust, understanding, and mutual support. Cultivating these qualities requires intentional effort and practice, but the rewards—strong, resilient relationships—are invaluable. Through consistent application of these principles, you can build a foundation of respect, trust, and empathy that will enrich your connections with others.

Its Always The Baby Steps.

The smaller steps people take often yield bigger dreams, but the limiting factor is consistency.

When it comes to etiquette, everyone is bound by it, and there is no way one can exist in this life without ethical principles acting upon them.

Life is like a plant that can only grow in fertile soils regardless of the type of fertilizers; however, the type of water and the frequency of watering affect its growth, no matter the quality and quantity of fertilizers used.

It's always better to remember to water our life frequently by practicing the etiquettes that make us beings of humanity rather than merely human beings.

These principles are like "diamonds" formed under the layers of the earth amidst high pressure and temperature near the earth's crust.

Diamonds are stable, priceless, and symbolize nobility and loyalty.

Sparkling when the light shines on them and harder to break and crush, they are magnificent and beautiful.

The four etiquettes of personal development or growth—gratitude, kindness, forgiveness, and self-care—are considered diamonds in human moral and ethical ways by the laws of nature.

They give the true definition of it all.

One must develop a routine to incorporate these principles into daily life and persist no matter the circumstances.

Setting aside a specific time each day for journaling and making it a habit to express gratitude before the last prayer, meals, or bedtime is a great way to start, as it allows for fewer disturbances and more sincerity.

By making it a regular practice, one can experience transformative effects on personal growth and development, leading to better and morally acceptable behavior or etiquette.

It's important to remember that developing a forgiving personality is a lengthy journey that requires extra effort, patience, and gratitude to celebrate each step toward a more compassionate and forgiving outlook on life.

The journey to self-care also requires intention and commitment.

It is not a luxury but a fundamental aspect of leading a fulfilling and balanced life.

People who practice self-care testify to gaining resilience, reducing stress, enhancing well-being, and expressing the best versions of themselves in all aspects of life, including relationships, work, and society.

Effective communication is not a one-time practice but rather a lifelong learning process.

One must seek opportunities to enhance communication skills through activities such as reading, attending workshops, and seminars, actively seeking feedback, and reflecting on ongoing improvement.

As people cultivate the power and skills in active listening, we will have communities that create spaces for everyone's voice, allowing them to be heard and understood.

An empathetic lifestyle is not just about solving other people's problems or making everything better for others.

It also extends to being a supportive, understanding, and validating person, which requires many other sets of skills such as respect, listening, kindness, self-reflection, compassion, and love.

Education and exposure to different perspectives play a significant role in developing a respectful character.

By learning about diverse cultures, histories, and experiences, one gains a better and more empathetic understanding, which fosters an appreciative and respectful approach toward others.

In summary, accountability etiquette is essential for professional success.

It builds trust, enhances performance, drives personal growth, fosters effective communication, and cultivates a culture of reliability and excellence.

By embracing accountability, professionals position themselves as valuable contributors, gain the respect of their peers and superiors, and create opportunities for advancement and long-term success in their careers.

Networking etiquette significantly impacts professional success.

By expanding opportunities, building relationships, sharing knowledge, seeking guidance, fostering collaboration, and enhancing visibility, individuals can leverage their networks to achieve career goals, access new opportunities, and accelerate their professional growth.

Networking is a powerful tool for professional success that should be approached with authenticity, professionalism, and a genuine desire to build meaningful connections.

Adaptability is a valuable skill that enables professionals to navigate complexities, seize opportunities, and continually adapt to the evolving demands of their careers.

In conclusion, the role of etiquette in human relationships cannot be overstated.

It is the invisible thread that binds us together, fostering respect, understanding, and harmony.

By practicing relationship etiquette, we can build and maintain strong, healthy connections in all areas of our lives—be it friendship, love, family, work, or community.

Reflecting on these principles and making a conscious effort to uphold them can transform our interactions and enrich our relationships.

This concludes our exploration of the profound impact of etiquette on personal and professional success.

By embracing these principles, we not only improve our own lives but also contribute to a more respectful and harmonious world.

Thank you for embarking on this journey with us.

Remember, it's the smaller steps that often yield the biggest dreams.

www.ingramcontent.com/pod-product-compliance
Lightning Source LLC
LaVergne TN
LVHW041038150826
845672LV00001B/380

* 9 7 9 8 8 9 6 9 9 0 1 8 5 *